Atlas of Brainy Challenges

Map It! ™

Volume 2

From America's #1 Road Atlas

RAND MCNALLY

Map It!™

Concept and Editorial Direction: Joan Sharp
Design: Dawne Lundahl
Writer: Mary Bunker
Design Production: Dawne Lundahl
Product Management Director: Jenny Thornton
Production: Carey Seren
Cartography: Gregory P. Babiak, Robert Ferry, Justin Griffin, Steve Wiertz, Thomas F. Vitacco

Published in U.S.A.
Printed in Canada
January 2020
PO# 71389
ISBN 0-528-01904-X

If you have any questions, concerns or even a compliment,
please visit us at randmcnally.com/tellrand or write to:
Rand McNally Consumer Affairs
P.O. Box 7600
Chicago, Illinois 60680-9915

randmcnally.com

Rand McNally *CarTainment*

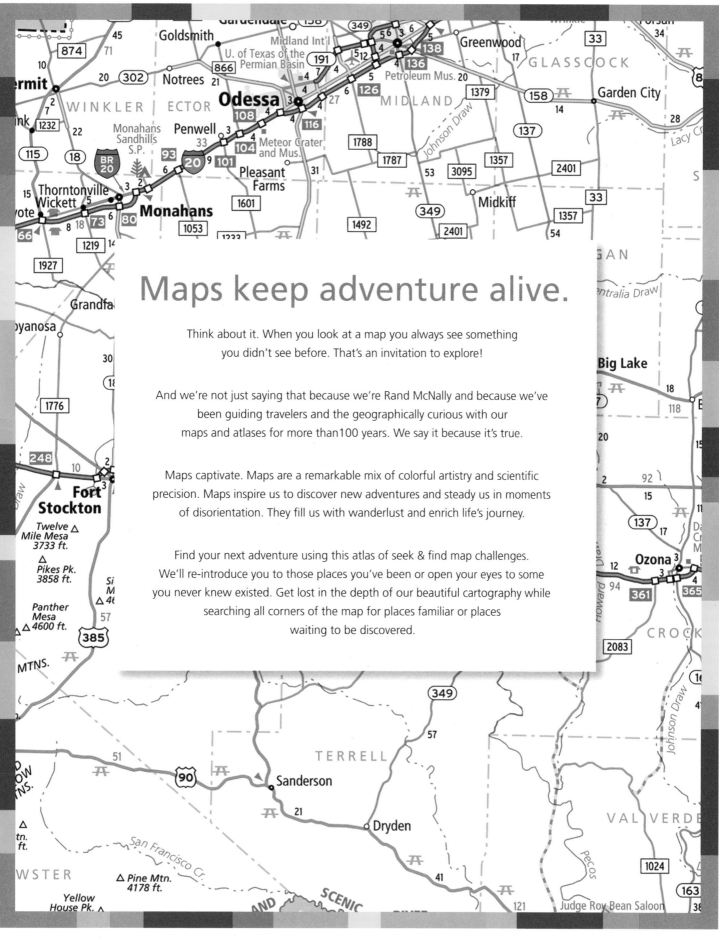

Maps keep adventure alive.

Think about it. When you look at a map you always see something you didn't see before. That's an invitation to explore!

And we're not just saying that because we're Rand McNally and because we've been guiding travelers and the geographically curious with our maps and atlases for more than 100 years. We say it because it's true.

Maps captivate. Maps are a remarkable mix of colorful artistry and scientific precision. Maps inspire us to discover new adventures and steady us in moments of disorientation. They fill us with wanderlust and enrich life's journey.

Find your next adventure using this atlas of seek & find map challenges. We'll re-introduce you to those places you've been or open your eyes to some you never knew existed. Get lost in the depth of our beautiful cartography while searching all corners of the map for places familiar or places waiting to be discovered.

Contents

Map Legend

Roads and related symbols

Limited-access, multilane highway—free; toll

New road (under construction as of press time)

Other multilane highway

Principal highway

Other through highway

Other road (conditions vary — local inquiry suggested)

Unpaved road (conditions vary — local inquiry suggested)

Ramp; one way route

Car ferry (with toll unless otherwise indicated on map)

Tunnel; mountain pass

Railroad; Intracoastal Waterway

Interstate highway; Interstate highway business route

U.S. highway; U.S. highway business route

Trans-Canada highway; Autoroute

Mexican highway or Central American highway

State/provincial highway; secondary state/provincial, or county highway

Great River Road; Great Lakes Circle Tour

Lewis & Clark Trail Highway; Lincoln Highway; Historic Route 66

Scenic route

Service area; toll booth or fee booth

Interchanges and exit numbers
For most states, the mileage between interchanges may be determined by subtracting one number from the other.

Highway distances (segments of one mile or less not shown):
Cumulative miles (red): the distance between arrows
Cumulative kilometers (blue): the distance between arrows
Intermediate miles (black): the distance between intersections & places

Comparative distance
1 mile = 1.609 kilometers   1 kilometer = 0.621 mile

Cities & towns size of type on map indicates relative population

National capital; state or provincial capital

County seat or independent city

City, town, or recognized place—incorporated; unincorporated

Urbanized area

Separate cities within metropolitan area

Parks, recreation areas, & other points of interest

National park

Other national park system location

National forest, national grassland, or city park; Wilderness area

State/provincial park system location; State/provincial forest

State/provincial park system location—with campsites; without campsites

Campsite; wayside or roadside park

Point of interest, historic site or monument

Airport

Building

Foot trail

Golf course or country club; ski area

Hospital or medical center

Military or governmental installation; military airport

Native American tribal lands

Ranger station

Rest area—with toilets; without toilets

Tourist information center; port of entry

Physical features

Mountain peak; highest point in state/province

Lake; intermittent lake; dry lake

River; intermittent river

Dam; swamp or mangrove swamp

Desert; glacier

Continental divide

Other symbols

Area shown in greater detail on inset map

Inset map page indicator (if not on same page)

County or parish boundary and name

State or provincial boundary

National boundary

Time zone boundary

Latitude; longitude

Map abbreviations

Listed below are some of the commonly used abbreviations on our maps. For a complete list of abbreviations that appear on the maps, go to www.randmcnally.com/ABBR.

Bfld.	Battlefield	N.P.	National Park
Cr.	Creek	N.R.A.	National Recreation Area
I.	Island	N.W.R.	National Wildlife Refuge
Int'l	International	S.H.S.	State Historic Site
L.	Lake	S.N.A.	State Natural Area
N.H.P.	National Historic Park	S.P.	State Park
N.H.S.	National Historic Site	S.R.A.	State Recreation Area
N.M.	National Monument	W.M.A.	Wildlife Management Area

Population figures used in this atlas are from the latest available census or are Census Bureau or Rand McNally estimates.
©2018 RM Acquisition, LLC d/b/a Rand McNally.

Let's get mapping!

The Rand McNally *Map It!*™ *Atlas of Brainy Challenges* puts your navigation skills to the test with 24 seek & find puzzles. Each puzzle uses a section of a state map from America's #1 Road Atlas.

Have fun ticking off the creatively cultivated and uniquely categorized puzzle challenges comprised of cities, towns and counties; lakes, ponds and rivers; parks and campgrounds—all unique to the state. Chances are you'll never look at a map the same way again!

How to *Map It!*™

Choose the state you'd like to explore, check out the puzzle challenges selected for each category listed, grab a pencil or highlighter, and get started. Once you seek a challenge on the map, *Map It!*™ with a circle or highlight, then jot down the coordinates next to the listing on the left hand page to mark the challenge as solved. Coordinates can be found using the letter and number grids that frame each map (we call this grid a "bingo.") For example, if a town named *Cranberry Lake* is on the list, it may be found in the coordinates B3, (as shown to the right.)

Helpful Tips

- Use the legend on page 4 to guide your search and to understand a map's pictorial language.

- Use a magnifying glass to take a deeper dive and get lost in the art and science of cartography.

- Some challenges are listed with an asterisk (*) to indicate duplicate locations on a map. Remember to seek for multiple coordinates!

- Note that all lakes and creeks are spelled as they appear on the map.

- State Forests will carry a suffix of S.F., State Recreation Areas have an S.R.A. suffix, but State Parks will not carry any suffix.

Check Your Work

Want to see if you've got it right? Are you stumped? Turn to pages 54-64 for puzzle solutions.

Towns
- ❏ Cranberry Lake   *B3*

Creeks & Rivers
- ❏ Pequest   *C1*

Lakes
- ❏ Budd Lake   *C3*

Villes
- ❏ Pottersville   *E3*

State Parks
- ❏ Swartswood   *A2*

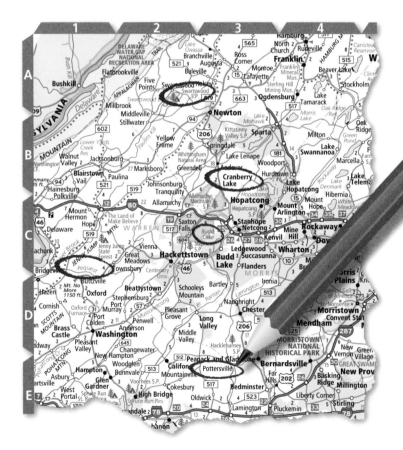

Nevada
The Silver State

You're in the desert. Driving outside Goldfield, NV. Is that a mirage? You wipe your eyes. No, it's more of a garage. Rising from the sand are over 40 rusting, cars, buses, vans and a milk truck, parked, stacked up or sticking up at odd angles from the ground. Called the International Car Forest of the Last Church, these junkers are now canvases for some crazy, thought-provoking art and sometimes backdrop for concerts. To see is to believe.

How To Map It!™
Use the list below to seek a challenge found on the map and cross it off as you go. **Instructions on page 5.**

Towns
- ☒ Goldfield *I,S*
- ❑ Ash Springs __ __
- ❑ Beowawe __ __
- ❑ Cherry Creek __ __
- ❑ Duckwater __ __
- ❑ Empire __ __
- ❑ Eureka __ __
- ❑ Gabbs __ __
- ❑ Gold Point __ __
- ❑ Hiko __ __
- ❑ Jarbridge __ __
- ❑ Lone __ __
- ❑ Lovelock __ __
- ❑ Manhattan __ __
- ❑ Nixon __ __
- ❑ Owyhee __ __
- ❑ Paradise Valley __ __
- ❑ Stagecoach __ __
- ❑ Warm Springs __ __

Creeks & Rivers
- ❑ Bull Creek __ __
- ❑ Bull Run __ __
- ❑ Dixie __ __
- ❑ Franklin __ __
- ❑ Hot Creek __ __
- ❑ *Humbolt __ __ ,
- ❑ Kings __ __
- ❑ Leonard __ __
- ❑ Maggie Cr. __ __
- ❑ Marys __ __
- ❑ Mud Meadow __ __
- ❑ Pine Cr. __ __
- ❑ *Quinn __ __ ,
     __ __
- ❑ Reese __ __
- ❑ Rock Creek __ __
- ❑ Spring Cr. __ __
- ❑ Susie Cr. __ __
- ❑ Walker __ __
- ❑ *White __ __ , __ __

Lakes
- ❑ Bishop Creek Reservoir __ __
- ❑ Carson Lake __ __
- ❑ Chimney Dam Res. __ __
- ❑ Desert Lake __ __
- ❑ Franklin Lake __ __
- ❑ Groom Lake __ __
- ❑ Lahontan Res. __ __
- ❑ Massacre Lake __ __
- ❑ Mud Lake __ __
- ❑ New Year Lake __ __
- ❑ Newark Lake __ __
- ❑ Pyramid Lake __ __
- ❑ Ruby Lake __ __
- ❑ Rye Patch Reservoir __ __
- ❑ Wild Horse Res. __ __
- ❑ Winnemucca Lake __ __
- ❑ Yucca Lake __ __

Mountains & Peaks
- ❑ Bald Mountain __ __
- ❑ Bald Mtn. __ __
- ❑ Bloody Run Pk. __ __
- ❑ Buffalo Mtn. __ __
- ❑ Cactus Pk. __ __
- ❑ Diamond Pk. __ __
- ❑ Disaster Peak __ __
- ❑ Emigrant Pass __ __
- ❑ Emigrant Pk. __ __
- ❑ Granite Pk. __ __
- ❑ Grapevine Pk. __ __
- ❑ Hot Springs Pk. __ __
- ❑ Ninemile Peak __ __
- ❑ Pah-Rum Pk. __ __
- ❑ Pancake Summit __ __
- ❑ Pilot Pk. __ __
- ❑ Shoshone Peak __ __
- ❑ Troy Pk. __ __

Counties
- ❑ Churchill __ __
- ❑ Douglas __ __
- ❑ Elko __ __
- ❑ Esmeralda __ __
- ❑ Eureka __ __
- ❑ Humboldt __ __
- ❑ Lander __ __
- ❑ Lyon __ __
- ❑ Mineral __ __
- ❑ Nye __ __
- ❑ Pershing __ __
- ❑ Storey __ __
- ❑ Washoe __ __
- ❑ White Pine __ __

* Multiple coordinates | Puzzle solutions pages 54-64

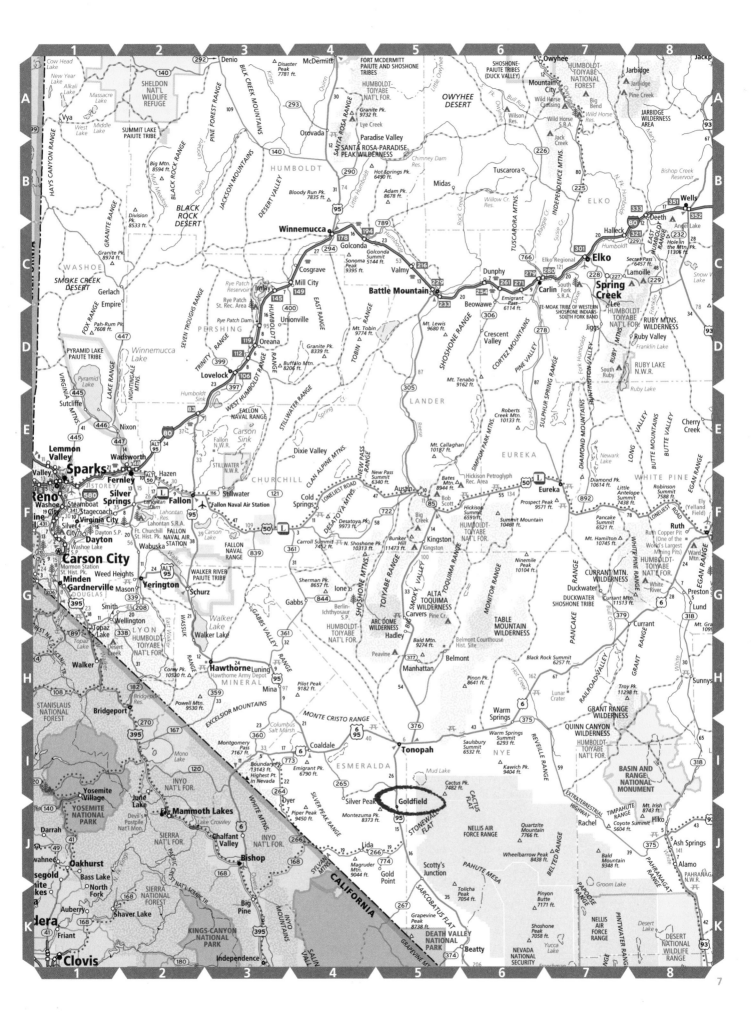

New Hampshire
The Granite State

Ever eaten an albacore sub? Ever been inside one?
In Portsmouth, NH, the U.S.S. Albacore, a 200-ft.,
decommissioned, Cold War, research submarine welcomes visitors in Albacore Park. Returned
to the city that built her, this stealth sub has secrets we'll never know but is now open to explore.
Sit at her helm, up periscope, spin dials, test the bunks and press buttons to hear former crews
talk of her adventures (the unclassified stuff of course.)

How To Map It!™

Use the list below to seek a challenge found on the map
and cross it off as you go. **Instructions on page 5.**

Towns	Creeks & Rivers	Lakes	Hills, Mills & Villes	State Parks
☒ Portsmouth I,7	❑ Ammonoosuc __ __	❑ Bellamy Res. __ __	❑ Bow Mills __ __	❑ Bear Brook __ __
❑ Albany __ __	❑ Ashuelot __ __	❑ Bow Lake __ __	❑ Bowkerville __ __	❑ Clough __ __
❑ Beebe River __ __	❑ Baker __ __	❑ Crystal Lake __ __	❑ Cornish Mills __ __	❑ Crawford Notch __ __
❑ Cascade __ __	❑ Chickwolnepy __ __	❑ Drew Lake __ __	❑ Danville __ __	❑ Echo Lake __ __
❑ Dorchester __ __	❑ Cold __ __	❑ Goose Pd. __ __	❑ Davisville __ __	❑ Ellacoya __ __
❑ Fabyan __ __	❑ Connecticut __ __	❑ Highland Lake __ __	❑ Drewsville __ __	❑ Forest Lake __ __
❑ Groveton __ __	❑ Contoocook __ __	❑ Island Pond __ __	❑ Gossville __ __	❑ Franconia Notch __ __
❑ Henniker __ __	❑ Ellis __ __	❑ Lake Tarleton __ __	❑ Greenville __ __	❑ Greenfield __ __
❑ Kelleys Corner __ __	❑ Exeter __ __	❑ Lake Wentworth __ __	❑ Harrisville __ __	❑ Kingston __ __
❑ Lyndeborough __ __	❑ Isrea __ __	❑ Mascoma L. __ __	❑ Hill __ __	❑ Monadnock __ __
❑ Milan __ __	❑ Mad __ __	❑ Newfound Lake __ __	❑ Kellyville __ __	❑ Moose Brook __ __
❑ Newmarket __ __	❑ Merrimack __ __	❑ Nubanusit Lake __ __	❑ Munsonville __ __	❑ Mt. Sunapee __ __
❑ Ossipee __ __	❑ Pemigewasset __ __	❑ Ossipee Lake __ __	❑ Orfordville __ __	❑ Pilsbury __ __
❑ Pembroke __ __	❑ Pine __ __	❑ Silver Lake __ __	❑ Parker Hill __ __	❑ Pisgah __ __
❑ Potter Place __ __	❑ Saco __ __	❑ Squam Lake __ __	❑ Sanbornville __ __	❑ Rollins __ __
❑ Sandwich __ __	❑ Smith __ __	❑ Success Pond __ __	❑ Snowville __ __	❑ Rye Harbor __ __
❑ Tilton __ __	❑ Souhegan __ __	❑ Sunapee Lake __ __	❑ Sugar Hill __ __	❑ Silver Lake __ __
❑ Unity __ __	❑ Sugar __ __	❑ Union L. __ __	❑ Waterville Valley __ __	❑ Wadleigh __ __
❑ Woodstock __ __	❑ Swift __ __	❑ Weare Reservoir __ __	❑ Westville __ __	❑ Wellington __ __

Puzzle solutions pages 54-64

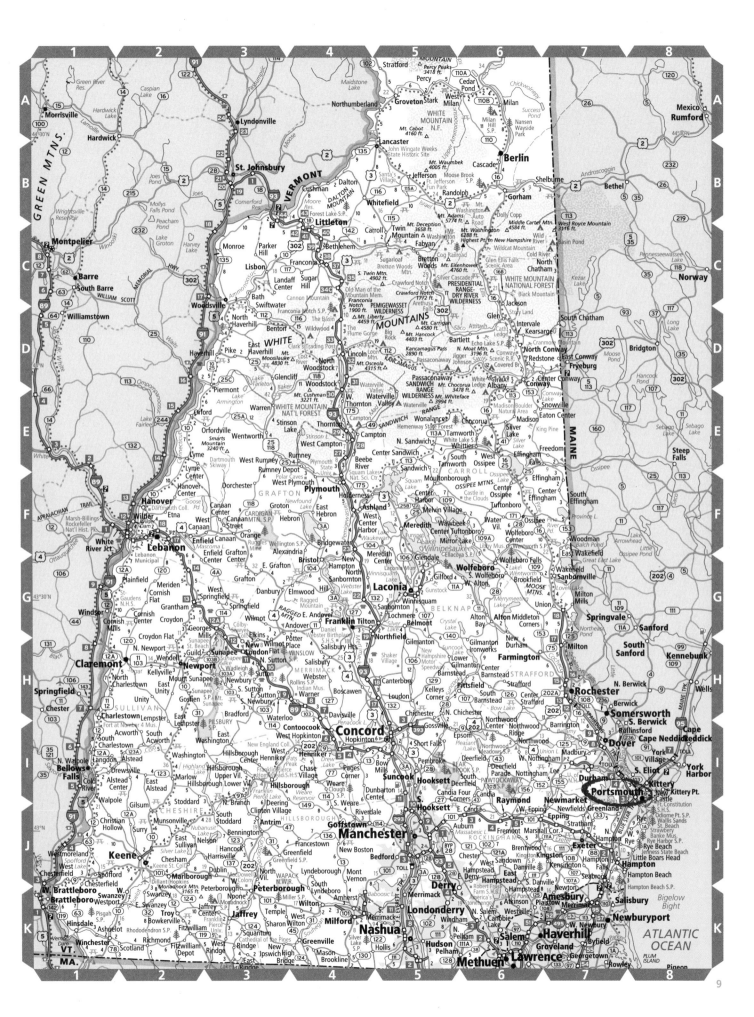

New Jersey
The Garden State

Play ball! Odds are, this familiar baseball call was first shouted at Elysian Fields in Hoboken, NJ where the 1846 Knickerbocker Baseball Club of New York played their first game against the New York Baseball Club. Today, at 11th and Washington Streets, The Birthplace of Baseball Monument marks the original spot of the field's diamond, along with four base markers at each corner of the intersection. Game for a visit?

How To Map It!™

Use the list below to seek a challenge found on the map and cross it off as you go. **Instructions on page 5.**

Towns

- ☒ Hoboken D,7
- ❏ Chambers Corners __ __
- ❏ Colts Neck __ __
- ❏ Cranberry Lake __ __
- ❏ Cream Ridge __ __
- ❏ Dutch Neck __ __
- ❏ Green Pond __ __
- ❏ Holiday City __ __
- ❏ Jobstown __ __
- ❏ Lake Como __ __
- ❏ Liberty Corner __ __
- ❏ Lincoln Park __ __
- ❏ Mount Airy __ __
- ❏ Mount Hope __ __
- ❏ Mount Pleasant __ __
- ❏ Short Hills __ __
- ❏ Vienna __ __
- ❏ Wickatunk __ __
- ❏ Windsor __ __
- ❏ Yellow Frame __ __

Creeks & Rivers

- ❏ Beaver Brook __ __
- ❏ Crosswicks Cr. __ __
- ❏ Delaware __ __
- ❏ Lamington __ __
- ❏ Metedeconk __ __
- ❏ Millstone __ __
- ❏ Musconetcong __ __
- ❏ Paulins Kill __ __
- ❏ Pequest __ __
- ❏ Ramapo __ __
- ❏ Rockaway __ __
- ❏ S. Br. Raritan __ __
- ❏ South __ __
- ❏ Stony Br. __ __
- ❏ Toms Cr. __ __
- ❏ Whippany __ __

Lakes

- ❏ Boonton Res. __ __
- ❏ Budd Lake __ __
- ❏ Canistear Reservoir __ __
- ❏ Clinton Res. __ __
- ❏ Echo L. __ __
- ❏ Green Pond __ __
- ❏ Lake Denmark __ __
- ❏ Lake Mohawk __ __
- ❏ Lake Owassa __ __
- ❏ Lake Tappan __ __
- ❏ Lower Yards Creek Res. __ __
- ❏ Mirror Lake __ __
- ❏ Oak Ridge Res. __ __
- ❏ Oradell Res. __ __
- ❏ Round Valley Res. __ __
- ❏ Splitrock Res. __ __
- ❏ Spruce Run Res. __ __
- ❏ Wanaque Reservoir __ __

Villes

- ❏ Branchville __ __
- ❏ Buttzville __ __
- ❏ Cherryville __ __
- ❏ Denville __ __
- ❏ Ewansville __ __
- ❏ Flatbrookville __ __
- ❏ Groveville __ __
- ❏ Jerseyville __ __
- ❏ Lawrenceville __ __
- ❏ Middleville __ __
- ❏ Morganville __ __
- ❏ Osbornsville __ __
- ❏ Pottersville __ __
- ❏ Robbinsville __ __
- ❏ Robertsville __ __
- ❏ Rudeville __ __
- ❏ Scobeyville __ __
- ❏ Titusville __ __
- ❏ Warrenville __ __

State Parks

- ❏ Allaire __ __
- ❏ Cheesequake __ __
- ❏ Delaware and Raritan Canal __ __
- ❏ Famy __ __
- ❏ Hacklebarney __ __
- ❏ Hopatcong __ __
- ❏ Jenny Jump State Forest __ __
- ❏ Kittatinny Valley __ __
- ❏ Long Pond Ironworks __ __
- ❏ Norvin Green __ __
- ❏ Princeton Bfld. __ __
- ❏ Ramapo Mountain
- ❏ Rancocas __ __
- ❏ Ringwood __ __
- ❏ Stephens __ __
- ❏ Swartswood __ __
- ❏ Voorhees __ __
- ❏ Washington Rock __ __

Puzzle solutions pages 54-64

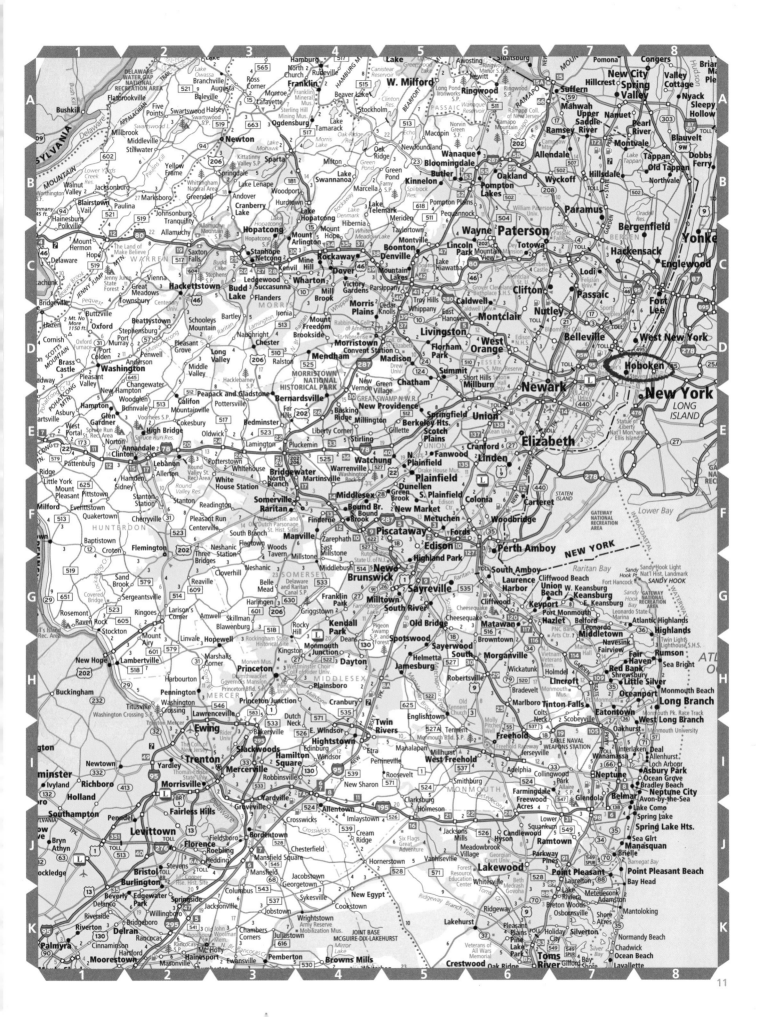

11

New York
The Empire State

Ever play the *Red Light Green Light* game? At the intersection of Milton Ave and Tompkins Street in Syracuse, NY, it's played *Green Light Red Light* because the traffic light colors are reversed. Irish families who settled this community didn't like British red being placed above Irish green. In 1925 the alderman secured a new light with green on top. It's the only traffic light of its kind and a symbol of Irish pride.

How To Map It!™
Use the list below to seek a challenge found on the map and cross it off as you go. **Instructions on page 5.**

Falls, Hills & Mills
- ☒ Syracuse I,2
- ☐ Brasher Falls ___ ___
- ☐ Brier Hill ___ ___
- ☐ Burrs Mills ___ ___
- ☐ Chase Mills ___ ___
- ☐ Chasm Falls ___ ___
- ☐ Clark Mills ___ ___
- ☐ Crary Mills ___ ___
- ☐ Delphi Falls ___ ___
- ☐ Evans Mills ___ ___
- ☐ Felts Mills ___ ___
- ☐ Hannawa Falls ___ ___
- ☐ Hope Falls ___ ___
- ☐ Lyons Falls ___ ___
- ☐ Newton Falls ___ ___
- ☐ Skaneateles Falls ___ ___
- ☐ St. Regis Falls ___ ___
- ☐ Stone Mills ___ ___
- ☐ Summer Hill ___ ___
- ☐ Tribes Hill ___ ___
- ☐ Vail Mills ___ ___

Creeks & Rivers
- ☐ Beaver ___ ___
- ☐ *Black ___ ___ , ___ ___ , ___ ___
- ☐ Black Cr. ___ ___
- ☐ Chateaugay ___ ___
- ☐ Cold ___ ___
- ☐ Deer ___ ___
- ☐ E. Canada Cr. ___ ___
- ☐ Indian ___ ___
- ☐ Mad ___ ___
- ☐ Moose ___ ___
- ☐ Oswegatchie ___ ___
- ☐ Otselic ___ ___
- ☐ Perch ___ ___
- ☐ *Raquette ___ ___ , ___ ___ , ___ ___
- ☐ S. Br. Grass ___ ___
- ☐ *Salmon ___ ___ , ___
- ☐ Spruce Cr. ___ ___
- ☐ St. Lawrence ___ ___
- ☐ Sugar ___ ___

Villes
- ☐ Bolgeville ___ ___
- ☐ Bouckville ___ ___
- ☐ Depauville ___ ___
- ☐ Edwardsville ___ ___
- ☐ Flackville ___ ___
- ☐ Garrattsville ___ ___
- ☐ Harrisville ___ ___
- ☐ Hornesville ___ ___
- ☐ La Fargeville ___ ___
- ☐ Lowville ___ ___
- ☐ Mannsville ___ ___
- ☐ Northville ___ ___
- ☐ Parishville ___ ___
- ☐ Pennellville ___ ___
- ☐ Richville ___ ___
- ☐ Tylersville ___ ___
- ☐ Unionville ___ ___
- ☐ Waterville ___ ___
- ☐ Westernville ___ ___

State Parks
- ☐ Battle Island ___ ___
- ☐ Burnham Point ___ ___
- ☐ Chittenango Falls ___ ___
- ☐ Coles Cr. ___ ___
- ☐ Delta Lake ___ ___
- ☐ Dewolf Pt. ___ ___
- ☐ Eel Weir ___ ___
- ☐ Fillmore Glen ___ ___
- ☐ Glimmerglass ___ ___
- ☐ Green Lakes ___ ___
- ☐ Higley Flow ___ ___
- ☐ Kring Point ___ ___
- ☐ Pixley Falls ___ ___
- ☐ Sandy Island Beach ___ ___
- ☐ Selkirk Shores ___ ___
- ☐ Southwick Beach ___ ___
- ☐ St. Lawrence ___ ___
- ☐ Verona Beach ___ ___
- ☐ Westcott Beach ___ ___

Lakes
- ☐ Ampersand Lake ___ ___
- ☐ Big Moose Lake ___ ___
- ☐ Bog Lake ___ ___
- ☐ Catlin L. ___ ___
- ☐ Cranberry Lake ___ ___
- ☐ Hinckley Res. ___ ___
- ☐ L. Bonaparte ___ ___
- ☐ L. Pleasant ___ ___
- ☐ L. Titus ___ ___
- ☐ Lake Eaton ___ ___
- ☐ Long Lake ___ ___
- ☐ Loon Lake ___ ___
- ☐ Mad ___ ___
- ☐ Mud L. ___ ___
- ☐ Norwood Lake ___ ___
- ☐ Oneida Lake ___ ___
- ☐ Perch L. ___ ___
- ☐ Rich L. ___ ___
- ☐ Woodhull Lake ___ ___
- ☐ Yellow L. ___ ___

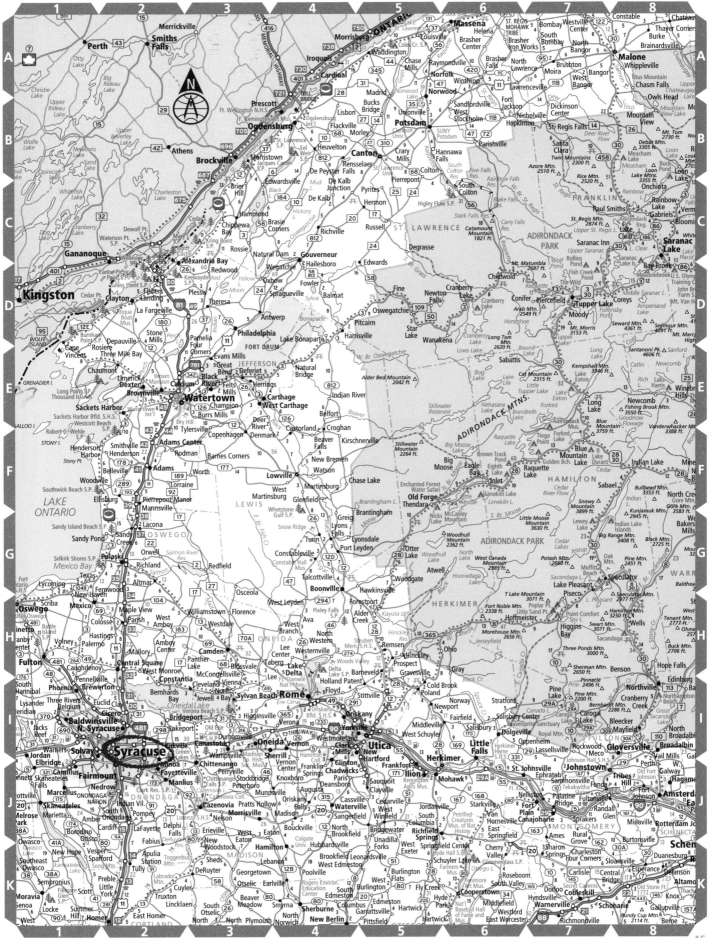

North Carolina
The Tar Heel State

You've got mail in Sunset Beach, NC. Well, you and everybody else. Just a short, beach stroll south sits the Kindred Spirit Mailbox on the shore of Bird Island Reserve. Inside you'll find a journal filled with travellers' stories, letters, hopes and wisdoms. Sit on the nearby bench to read and then share a message of your own. For 35+ years the mailbox has drawn kindred spirits from around the world who leave words of encouragement for all. No stamps needed.

How To Map It!™

Use the list below to seek a challenge found on the map and cross it off as you go. **Instructions on page 5.**

Burgs & Hills

- ☒ Sunset Beach K,6
- ☐ Abbottsburg __ __
- ☐ Arran Hills __ __
- ☐ Bethel Hill __ __
- ☐ Chapel Hill __ __
- ☐ Jackson Hill __ __
- ☐ Louisburg __ __
- ☐ New Hill __ __
- ☐ Oregon Hill __ __
- ☐ Parkersburg __ __
- ☐ Pink Hill __ __
- ☐ Prospect Hill __ __
- ☐ Rose Hill __ __
- ☐ Salemburg __ __
- ☐ Snow Hill __ __
- ☐ Stantonsburg __ __
- ☐ Williamsburg __ __

Creeks & Rivers

- ☐ Black __ __
- ☐ *Cape Fear __ __ ,
  __ __
- ☐ Colly Cr. __ __
- ☐ Dan __ __
- ☐ Deep __ __
- ☐ Fishing Cr. __ __
- ☐ Flat __ __
- ☐ Haw __ __
- ☐ Lumber __ __
- ☐ N.E. Cape Fear __ __
- ☐ Neuse __ __
- ☐ Six Runs Cr. __ __
- ☐ *South __ __ ,
- ☐ Tar __ __

Villes

- ☐ Allensville __ __
- ☐ Ansonville __ __
- ☐ Autryville __ __
- ☐ Barnesville __ __
- ☐ Brinkleyville __ __
- ☐ Casville __ __
- ☐ Centerville __ __
- ☐ Franklinville __ __
- ☐ Johnsonville __ __
- ☐ Kimesville __ __
- ☐ Mapleville __ __
- ☐ Morrisville __ __
- ☐ Pikeville __ __
- ☐ Prestonville __ __
- ☐ Proctorville __ __
- ☐ Townsville __ __
- ☐ Yanceyville __ __

Lakes

- ☐ Badin L. __ __
- ☐ Bay Tree Lake __ __
- ☐ Belews L. __ __
- ☐ Blewett Falls
  Lake __ __
- ☐ Falls Lake __ __
- ☐ High Rock L. __ __
- ☐ Horseshoe Lake __ __
- ☐ Hyco Lake __ __
- ☐ L. Tillery __ __
- ☐ L. Townsend __ __
- ☐ Lake Gaston __ __
- ☐ Lake Michie __ __
- ☐ Lake Waccamaw
  __ __
- ☐ Little Singletary L.
  __ __
- ☐ White Lake __ __

Counties

- ☐ Bladen __ __
- ☐ Brunswick __ __
- ☐ Caswell __ __
- ☐ Columbus __ __
- ☐ Durham __ __
- ☐ Guilford __ __
- ☐ Harnett __ __
- ☐ Hoke __ __
- ☐ Moore __ __
- ☐ Nash __ __
- ☐ Orange __ __
- ☐ Randolph __ __
- ☐ Richmond __ __
- ☐ Sampson __ __
- ☐ Scotland __ __
- ☐ Vance __ __
- ☐ Wayne __ __

* Multiple coordinates | Puzzle solutions pages 54-64

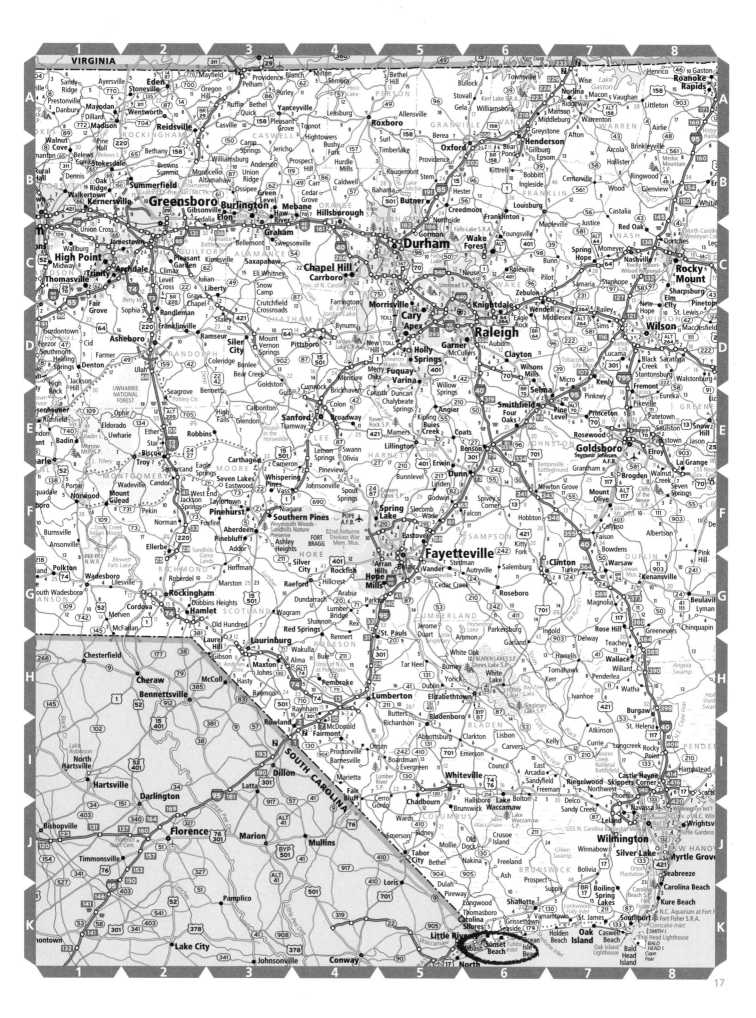

North Dakota
The Peace Garden State

They (whoever they are) say old cowboys never die, they simply ride away. But in North Dakota's Bismarck-Mandan area, the son of beloved rancher created a memorial that will ride on forever. Up on a hill off of old Highway 10, anchored to the ground, stand over 30 life-size, sculpted-steel, silhouette cutouts of cowboys on horseback moving cattle across the ridge. Tip your hat to his dad, he's the cowboy in front.

How To Map It!™

Use the list below to seek a challenge found on the map and cross it off as you go. **Instructions on page 5.**

His Town
- ☒ Bismarck I,1
- ☐ Adrian __ __
- ☐ Arthur __ __
- ☐ Barney __ __
- ☐ Barton __ __
- ☐ Calvin __ __
- ☐ Clifford __ __
- ☐ Clyde __ __
- ☐ Elliott __ __
- ☐ Guthrie __ __
- ☐ Horace __ __
- ☐ Hunter __ __
- ☐ Jessie __ __
- ☐ Leonard __ __
- ☐ Leroy __ __
- ☐ Milton __ __
- ☐ Mylo __ __
- ☐ Russell __ __
- ☐ Sheldon __ __

Her Town
- ☐ Alice __ __
- ☐ Aneta __ __
- ☐ Ashley __ __
- ☐ Crystal __ __
- ☐ Dazey __ __
- ☐ Flora __ __
- ☐ Gardena __ __
- ☐ Hannah __ __
- ☐ Hope __ __
- ☐ Juanita __ __
- ☐ Kathryn __ __
- ☐ Marion __ __
- ☐ McKenzie __ __
- ☐ Medina __ __
- ☐ Olga __ __
- ☐ Page __ __
- ☐ Sharon __ __
- ☐ Silva __ __
- ☐ Verona __ __

Lakes
- ☐ Arrowwood Lake __ __
- ☐ Beaver Lake __ __
- ☐ Blue Lake __ __
- ☐ Cranberry Lake __ __
- ☐ Crooked Lake __ __
- ☐ Dry Lake __ __
- ☐ Green Lake __ __
- ☐ Horsehead Lake __ __
- ☐ Lake George __ __
- ☐ Lake Tewaukon __ __
- ☐ *Long Lake __ __, __ __
- ☐ North Lake __ __
- ☐ Rock Lake __ __
- ☐ Round Lake __ __
- ☐ Rush Lake __ __
- ☐ Smoky Lake __ __
- ☐ Strawberry Lake __ __
- ☐ Stump Lake __ __
- ☐ Turtle Lake __ __

Creeks & Rivers
- ☐ Beaver Cr. __ __
- ☐ Elm __ __
- ☐ Forest __ __
- ☐ Goose __ __
- ☐ *James __ __ , __ __
- ☐ Maple __ __
- ☐ *Missouri __ __ , __ __
- ☐ Ox Cr. __ __
- ☐ Pipestem Cr. __ __
- ☐ *Red __ __ , __ __ , __ __
- ☐ Rush __ __
- ☐ S. Br. Park __ __
- ☐ *Sheyenne __ __ , __ __
- ☐ Souris __ __
- ☐ Tongue __ __
- ☐ Wild Rice __ __
- ☐ Willow Cr. __ __

Counties
- ☐ Barnes __ __
- ☐ Bottineau __ __
- ☐ Cavalier __ __
- ☐ Dickey __ __
- ☐ Eddy __ __
- ☐ Emmons __ __
- ☐ Foster __ __
- ☐ Grand Forks __ __
- ☐ Kidder __ __
- ☐ Logan __ __
- ☐ McHenry __ __
- ☐ Nelson __ __
- ☐ Pierce __ __
- ☐ Richland __ __
- ☐ Steele __ __
- ☐ Towner __ __
- ☐ Traill __ __
- ☐ Walsh __ __
- ☐ Wells __ __

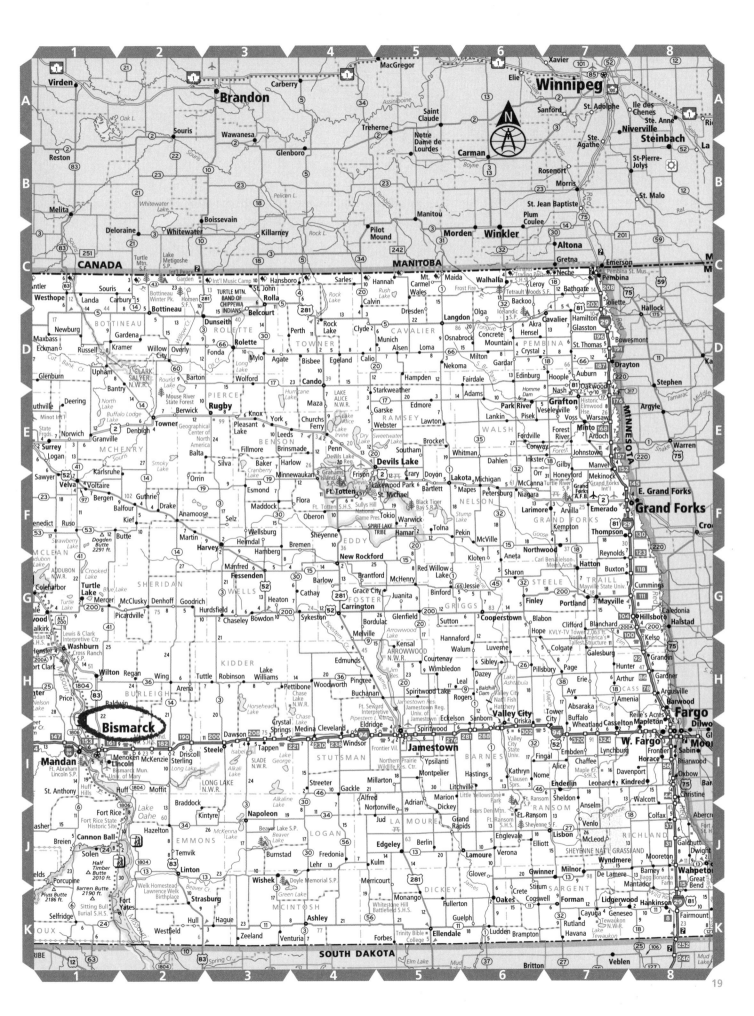

Ohio
The Buckeye State

Ohio is home to eight U.S. Presidents: W. Harrison, Grant, Hayes, Garfield, B. Harrison, McKinley, Taft, and Harding. Birthplaces, museums, libraries and monuments welcome visitors. But, if you're in Delaware, OH, prepare to drop your jaw. It was here, in 1926 that the birthplace of 19th President Rutherford B. Hayes was demolished and replaced with a plaque. And where today the plaque shares its spot with (*wait for it*) a gas station. Yep. This tank's for you Rutherford.

How To Map It!™

Use the list below to seek a challenge found on the map and cross it off as you go. **Instructions on page 5.**

Towns

- ☒ Delaware ⊐,6
- ❑ Africa __ __
- ❑ Berlin Hts. __ __
- ❑ Denmark __ __
- ❑ Havana __ __
- ❑ Kansas __ __
- ❑ Milan __ __
- ❑ Nevada __ __
- ❑ New California __ __
- ❑ New Hampshire __ __
- ❑ New Washington __ __
- ❑ North Baltimore __ __
- ❑ Oregon __ __
- ❑ Peru __ __
- ❑ Rome __ __
- ❑ Rushsylvania __ __
- ❑ Santa Fe __ __
- ❑ Texas __ __
- ❑ Waldo __ __

Creeks & Rivers

- ❑ Alum __ __
- ❑ Auglaize __ __
- ❑ Bad __ __
- ❑ Big Walnut __ __
- ❑ Clear Fk. __ __
- ❑ Honey Creek __ __
- ❑ Huron __ __
- ❑ Kokosing __ __
- ❑ Little Scioto __ __
- ❑ Maumee __ __
- ❑ Middle Br. Portage __ __
- ❑ Mill Creek __ __
- ❑ Ottawa __ __
- ❑ Portage __ __
- ❑ Rush __ __
- ❑ *Sandusky __ __ ,
- ❑ *Scioto __ __ , __ __
- ❑ Toussaint Cr. __ __

Lakes

- ❑ Alum Cr. L. __ __
- ❑ Clear Fork Reservoir __ __
- ❑ Delaware Lake __ __
- ❑ Hoover Res. __ __
- ❑ Indian L. __ __
- ❑ Kiser L. __ __
- ❑ O'Shaughnessy Res. __ __

State Parks

- ❑ Alum Cr. __ __
- ❑ Catawba I. __ __
- ❑ Crane Creek __ __
- ❑ Delaware __ __
- ❑ East Harbor __ __
- ❑ Indian I. __ __
- ❑ Kelleys I. __ __
- ❑ Maumee Bay __ __
- ❑ Middle Bass I. __ __
- ❑ Mt. Gilead __ __
- ❑ Van Buren __ __

Villes

- ❑ Bloomingville __ __
- ❑ Bloomville __ __
- ❑ Celeryville __ __
- ❑ Deweyville __ __
- ❑ Eagleville __ __
- ❑ Epsyville __ __
- ❑ Fitchville __ __
- ❑ Hoytville __ __
- ❑ Huntsville __ __
- ❑ Leesville __ __
- ❑ Logansville __ __
- ❑ Marysville __ __
- ❑ McCutchenville __ __
- ❑ Millersville __ __
- ❑ Monroeville __ __
- ❑ Pemberville __ __
- ❑ Rollersville __ __
- ❑ Waterville __ __
- ❑ Woodville __ __

Counties

- ❑ Allen __ __
- ❑ Auglaize __ __
- ❑ Crawford __ __
- ❑ Delaware __ __
- ❑ Erie __ __
- ❑ Hancock __ __
- ❑ Hardin __ __
- ❑ Henry __ __
- ❑ Huron __ __
- ❑ Logan __ __
- ❑ Lucas __ __
- ❑ Marion __ __
- ❑ Morrow __ __
- ❑ Ottawa __ __
- ❑ Richland __ __
- ❑ Seneca __ __
- ❑ Union __ __
- ❑ Wood __ __
- ❑ Wyandot __ __

* Multiple coordinates | Puzzle solutions pages 54-64

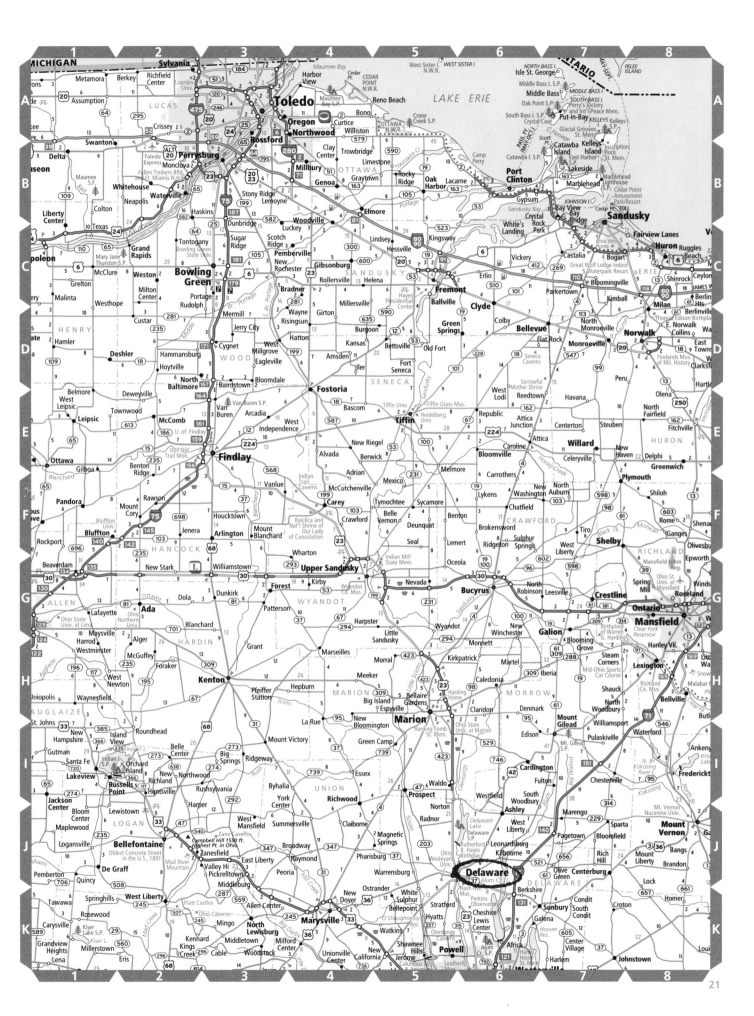

Ohio
The Buckeye State

How's that nursery rhyme go? "A-tisket, a-tasket, a seven-story basket." That's exactly how it goes in Newark, OH when you're standing in front of a giant woven market basket/office building that is 160 times bigger than the kind you carry, handles and all. Built in 1997, it was once the HQ of the Longaberger Basket Company and is still today, the world's largest basket. Just don't try skipping off to market with it.

How To Map It!™

Use the list below to seek a challenge found on the map and cross it off as you go. **Instructions on page 5.**

Towns	Creeks & Rivers	Lakes	Villes	State Parks
☒ Newark A,7	❏ Alum __ __	❏ Choctaw __ __	❏ Andersonville __ __	❏ Brush Cr. S.F. __ __
❏ Amity __ __	❏ Baker Fk. __ __	❏ Deer Cr. L. __ __	❏ Ashville __ __	❏ Buckeye Lake __ __
❏ Cook __ __	❏ Big Darby __ __	❏ Dillon L. __ __	❏ Dyesville __ __	❏ Burr Oak Cove __ __
❏ Dry Run __ __	❏ Deer __ __	❏ Hargus L. __ __	❏ Georgesville __ __	❏ Deer Cr. __ __
❏ Friendship __ __	❏ Hocking __ __	❏ Jackson Lake __ __	❏ Haydenville __ __	❏ Dillon __ __
❏ Hitchcock __ __	❏ Leading Cr. __ __	❏ L. Hope __ __	❏ Jacksonville __ __	❏ Great Seal __ __
❏ Hooker __ __	❏ Licking __ __	❏ L. Logan __ __	❏ Kirkersville __ __	❏ Hocking Hills __ __
❏ Kinnikinnick __ __	❏ Little Darby __ __	❏ L. Vesuvius __ __	❏ Langsville __ __	❏ Jackson Lake __ __
❏ Locust Grove __ __	❏ Moxahala __ __	❏ L. White __ __	❏ Lockville __ __	❏ L. Alma __ __
❏ Moxahala __ __	❏ Ohio __ __	❏ Paint Cr. L. __ __	❏ Matville __ __	❏ L. Hope __ __
❏ Ohio Furnace __ __	❏ Paint Cr. __ __	❏ Rocky Fk. L. __ __	❏ Mercerville __ __	❏ L. Logan __ __
❏ Patriot __ __	❏ Raccoon Cr. __ __	❏ Roosevelt L. __ __	❏ Nelsonville __ __	❏ Madison L. __ __
❏ Pleasant Corners __ __	❏ Rattlesnake __ __	❏ Ross L. __ __	❏ Outville __ __	❏ Perry St. For. __ __
❏ Redtown __ __	❏ Rush Cr. __ __	❏ Turkey Cr. L. __ __	❏ Powellsville __ __	❏ Pike Lake __ __
❏ Squirrel Town __ __	❏ Salt Cr. __ __	❏ Tycoon L. __ __	❏ Rubyville __ __	❏ Rocky Fk. __ __
❏ Tobosco __ __	❏ Scioto __ __		❏ Rushville __ __	❏ Scioto Trail __ __
❏ Unity __ __	❏ Sunday __ __		❏ Shadeville __ __	❏ Shawnee __ __
❏ White Cottage __ __	❏ Walnut Cr. __ __		❏ Thornville __ __	❏ Tar Hollow S.F. __ __
			❏ Wrightsville __ __	❏ Zeleski S.F. __ __

* Multiple coordinates | Puzzle solutions pages 54-64

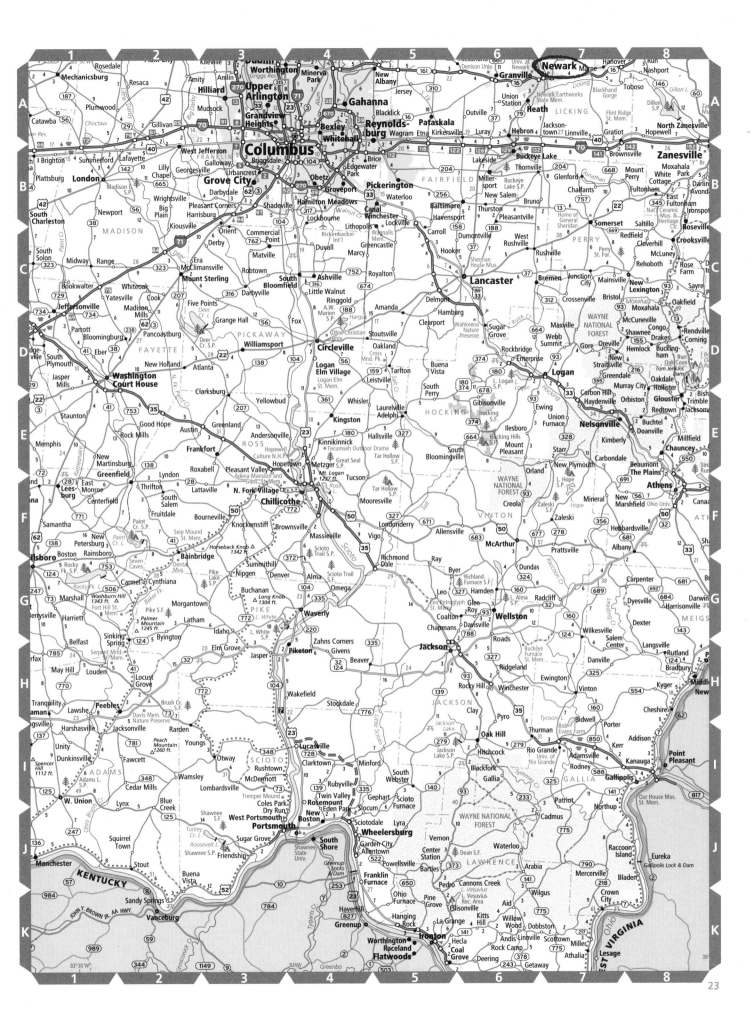

Oklahoma
The Sooner State

Ever feel like you're just talking to yourself? That's OK in downtown Tulsa, OK while you're standing in the small, concrete circle known as the Center of the Universe. This spot is an acoustic phenomenon where you can speak out loud and hear your voice echo back several times louder in your head, while no one near you hears a thing. There are plenty of theories as to how this happens, but one thing's for sure, it's always fun and a little freaky.

How To Map It!™

Use the list below to seek a challenge found on the map and cross it off as you go. **Instructions on page 5.**

Her Town
- ☒ Tulsa C, 4
- ☐ Adair __ __
- ☐ Avery __ __
- ☐ Bernice __ __
- ☐ Chelsea __ __
- ☐ Christie __ __
- ☐ Hanna __ __
- ☐ Joy __ __
- ☐ Katie __ __
- ☐ Lula __ __
- ☐ Mazie __ __
- ☐ Octavia __ __
- ☐ Oleta __ __
- ☐ Ramona __ __
- ☐ Rose __ __
- ☐ Savanna __ __
- ☐ Vera __ __
- ☐ Vivian __ __
- ☐ Zoe __ __

State Parks
- ☐ Arrowhead __ __
- ☐ Boggy Depot __ __
- ☐ Brushy Lake __ __
- ☐ Disney Little Blue __ __
- ☐ Dripping Springs __ __
- ☐ Greenleaf __ __
- ☐ Hochatown __ __
- ☐ Hugo Lake __ __
- ☐ Keystone __ __
- ☐ Lake Thunderbird __ __
- ☐ Lake Wister __ __
- ☐ Okmulgee __ __
- ☐ Osage Hills __ __
- ☐ Robbers Cave __ __
- ☐ Sequoyah Bay __ __
- ☐ Snowdale __ __
- ☐ Tenkiller __ __
- ☐ Walnut Cr. __ __

Counties
- ☐ Adair __ __
- ☐ Bryan __ __
- ☐ Choctaw __ __
- ☐ Craig __ __
- ☐ Creek __ __
- ☐ Delaware __ __
- ☐ Garvin __ __
- ☐ Haskell __ __
- ☐ Johnston __ __
- ☐ Kay __ __
- ☐ Latimer __ __
- ☐ Le Flore __ __
- ☐ Love __ __
- ☐ Noble __ __
- ☐ Okmulgee __ __
- ☐ Pittsburg __ __
- ☐ Pushmataha __ __
- ☐ Rogers __ __
- ☐ Seminole __ __

His Town
- ☐ Allen __ __
- ☐ Brent __ __
- ☐ Calvin __ __
- ☐ Dale __ __
- ☐ Dustin __ __
- ☐ Francis __ __
- ☐ Gene Autry __ __
- ☐ Geonard __ __
- ☐ Grant __ __
- ☐ Grayson __ __
- ☐ Hugo __ __
- ☐ Leon __ __
- ☐ Leonard __ __
- ☐ Mason __ __
- ☐ Perry __ __
- ☐ Preston __ __
- ☐ Stuart __ __
- ☐ Tom __ __
- ☐ Troy __ __

Lakes
- ☐ Birch Lake __ __
- ☐ Copan Lake __ __
- ☐ Eufaula Lake __ __
- ☐ Ft. Gibson Lake __ __
- ☐ Heyburn Lake __ __
- ☐ Hugo Lake __ __
- ☐ Kaw Lake __ __
- ☐ Lake Arcadia __ __
- ☐ Lake McAlester __ __
- ☐ Lake Murray __ __
- ☐ Lake Thunderbird __ __
- ☐ McGee Creek Lake __ __
- ☐ Oologah Lake __ __
- ☐ Pine Creek Lake __ __
- ☐ Sardis Lake __ __
- ☐ Skiatook Lake __ __
- ☐ Sooner Lake __ __
- ☐ Tenkiller Ferry Lake __ __
- ☐ Wister Lake __ __

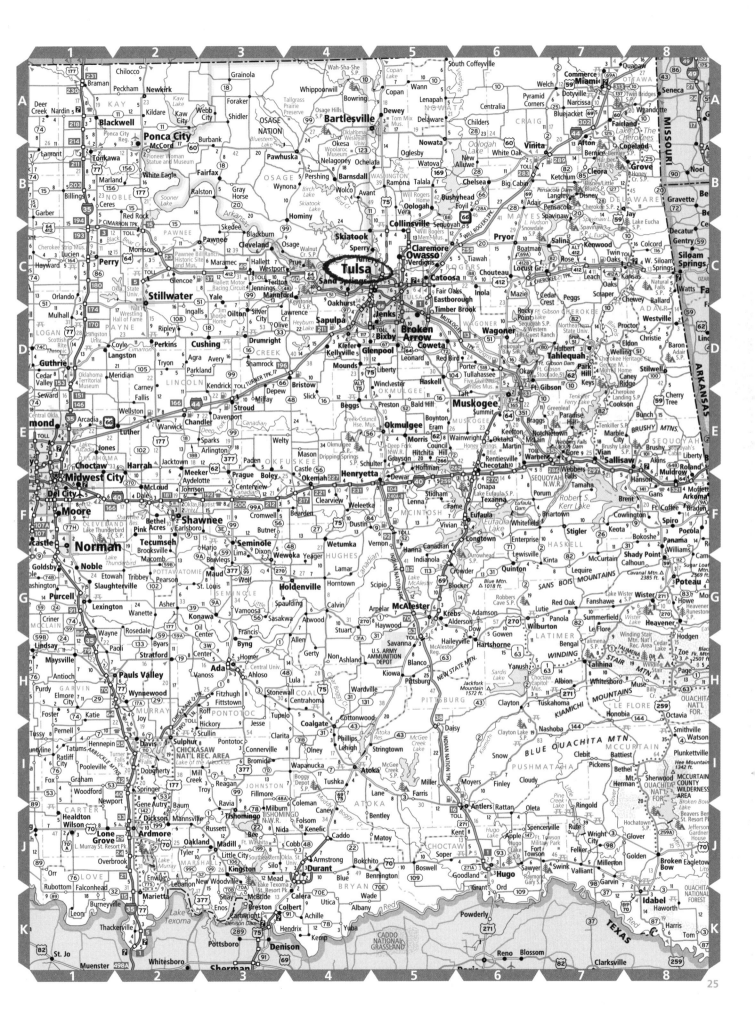

Oregon
The Beaver State

"Holy sinkhole Batman" (*make that Thor.*) Near Yachats, OR at the Cape Perpetua coastline is the breathtaking Thor's Well. It looks like a hole in the sea created by the hammer of a mythological god. About 10-feet across and 20-feet down, this collapsed sea cave perpetually fills and empties with Pacific waves and is most impressive at high tide when overflowing and erupting to heights of 20 feet. Superheroes not on duty, please view safely from the observation deck.

How To Map It!™
Use the list below to seek a challenge found on the map and cross it off as you go. **Instructions on page 5.**

Towns
- ☒ Yachats D,2
- ☐ Aumsville ___ ___
- ☐ Beaver Marsh ___ ___
- ☐ Crabtree ___ ___
- ☐ Crow ___ ___
- ☐ Eagle Point ___ ___
- ☐ Elk City ___ ___
- ☐ Elkton ___ ___
- ☐ Falcon Hts. ___ ___
- ☐ Finn Rock ___ ___
- ☐ Kernville ___ ___
- ☐ Otter Rock ___ ___
- ☐ Seal Rock ___ ___
- ☐ Sodaville ___ ___
- ☐ Three Lynx ___ ___
- ☐ Wilderville ___ ___
- ☐ Wolf Creek ___ ___
- ☐ Wren ___ ___

Rivers
- ☐ Annie ___ ___
- ☐ Applegate ___ ___
- ☐ Big ___ ___
- ☐ Calapooia ___ ___
- ☐ Clackamas ___ ___
- ☐ Deschutes ___ ___
- ☐ Illinois ___ ___
- ☐ Jenny ___ ___
- ☐ Little ___ ___
- ☐ Lost ___ ___
- ☐ Paulina ___ ___
- ☐ Pudding ___ ___
- ☐ *Rogue ___ ___ , ___ ___
- ☐ Sharps ___ ___
- ☐ Silver ___ ___
- ☐ Umpqua ___ ___
- ☐ Warm Springs ___ ___
- ☐ White ___ ___

Campsites
- ☐ Beaver Sulphur ___ ___
- ☐ Bogus Creek ___ ___
- ☐ Cedar Creek ___ ___
- ☐ Devils Lake ___ ___
- ☐ Dutch Oven ___ ___
- ☐ Eagle Rock ___ ___
- ☐ Frog Lake ___ ___
- ☐ Horse Creek ___ ___
- ☐ Horsefall ___ ___
- ☐ Lagoon ___ ___
- ☐ Lost Prairie ___ ___
- ☐ Paradise ___ ___
- ☐ Quosatana ___ ___
- ☐ Rainbow Bay ___ ___
- ☐ Squaw Lake ___ ___
- ☐ Threehorn ___ ___
- ☐ Trout Creek ___ ___
- ☐ Whiskey Springs ___ ___

Lakes
- ☐ Aspen Lake ___ ___
- ☐ Blue River Lake ___ ___
- ☐ Crater Lake ___ ___
- ☐ Dorena Lake ___ ___
- ☐ Fern Ridge Lake ___ ___
- ☐ Fish Lake ___ ___
- ☐ Foster Lake ___ ___
- ☐ Hyatt Res. ___ ___
- ☐ Lake Billy Chinook ___ ___
- ☐ Lava Lake ___ ___
- ☐ Lost Creek Lake ___ ___
- ☐ Siltcoos Lake ___ ___
- ☐ Suttle Lake ___ ___
- ☐ Tenmile Lake ___ ___
- ☐ Waldo Lake ___ ___

State Parks
- ☐ Alderwood St. Wayside ___ ___
- ☐ Beverly Beach ___ ___
- ☐ Cascadia ___ ___
- ☐ Detroit Lake S.R.A. ___ ___
- ☐ Elijah Bristow ___ ___
- ☐ Harris Beach ___ ___
- ☐ LaPine ___ ___
- ☐ Otter Point St. Rec. Site ___ ___
- ☐ Robert Straub ___ ___
- ☐ Silver Falls ___ ___
- ☐ Sunset Bay ___ ___
- ☐ The Cove Palisades ___ ___
- ☐ Tumalo ___ ___
- ☐ Val. of the Rogue ___ ___
- ☐ Yachats St. Rec Area ___ ___

* Multiple coordinates | Puzzle solutions pages 54-64

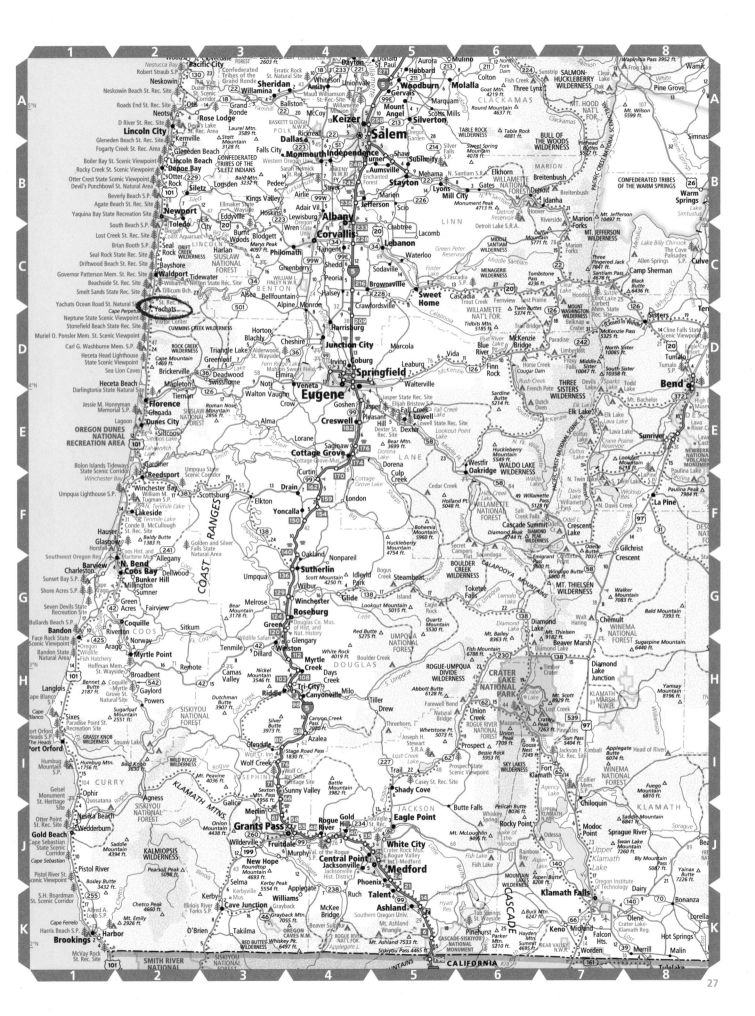

Pennsylvania
The Keystone State

Philadelphia's got the Liberty Bell, but some friends in Dauphin, PA felt their town needed something, too. So one night they took the liberty of planting a 25-foot replica of The Statue of Liberty on top an old stone bridge piling in the middle of the Susquehanna River. Created to celebrate Lady Liberty's 1986 centennial, the town kept it standing. When the homemade mini fell in a storm they built a new, more durable Lady who continues to welcome the masses on Route 322.

How To Map It!™
Use the list below to seek a challenge found on the map and cross it off as you go. **Instructions on page 5.**

Hills & Mills
- ☒ Dauphin I,3
- ☐ Balls Mills ___ ___
- ☐ Bunker Hill ___ ___
- ☐ Camp Hill ___ ___
- ☐ Cuba Mills ___ ___
- ☐ Donnally Mills ___ ___
- ☐ Globe Mills ___ ___
- ☐ Jersey Mills ___ ___
- ☐ Marsh Hill ___ ___
- ☐ Oakland Mills ___ ___
- ☐ Oregon Hill ___ ___
- ☐ Pond Hill ___ ___
- ☐ Russell Hill ___ ___
- ☐ Sand Hill ___ ___
- ☐ Spruce Hill ___ ___
- ☐ State Hill ___ ___
- ☐ Summer Hill ___ ___
- ☐ Terre Hill ___ ___

Villes
- ☐ Brandonville ___ ___
- ☐ Collomsville ___ ___
- ☐ Danville ___ ___
- ☐ Eatonville ___ ___
- ☐ Farmersville ___ ___
- ☐ Forksville ___ ___
- ☐ Grantville ___ ___
- ☐ Huntsville ___ ___
- ☐ Idaville ___ ___
- ☐ Koonsville ___ ___
- ☐ Larksville ___ ___
- ☐ Mainville ___ ___
- ☐ Millville ___ ___
- ☐ Perryville ___ ___
- ☐ Quiggleville ___ ___
- ☐ Rockville ___ ___
- ☐ Shellsville ___ ___
- ☐ Tylersville ___ ___
- ☐ Waterville ___ ___
- ☐ Wellsville ___ ___

Creeks & Rivers
- ☐ *Buffalo Cr. ___ ,
- ☐ Bowman Cr. ___ ___
- ☐ Catawissa Cr. ___ ___
- ☐ Clark Cr. ___ ___
- ☐ Fishing Cr. ___ ___
- ☐ Huntington Cr. ___ ___
- ☐ Jacks Cr. ___ ___
- ☐ Larrys Cr. ___ ___
- ☐ Lick Run ___ ___
- ☐ Little Juniatá Cr. ___ ___
- ☐ Loyalsock Cr. ___ ___
- ☐ Lycoming Cr. ___ ___
- ☐ Mahanoy Cr. ___ ___
- ☐ Penns Cr. ___ ___
- ☐ Roaring Cr. ___ ___
- ☐ Schuylkill ___ ___
- ☐ Swatara Cr. ___ ___
- ☐ White Deer Cr. ___ ___
- ☐ Wiconisco Cr. ___ ___

State Parks
- ☐ Bald Eagle S.F. ___ ___
- ☐ Colonel Denning ___ ___
- ☐ Gifford Pinchot ___ ___
- ☐ Little Buffalo ___ ___
- ☐ Little Pine ___ ___
- ☐ Locust Lake ___ ___
- ☐ Milton ___ ___
- ☐ Moon Lake S.F. ___ ___
- ☐ Nescopeck ___ ___
- ☐ Pine Grv. Furnace ___ ___
- ☐ Poe Paddy ___ ___
- ☐ Ravensburg ___ ___
- ☐ Reeds Gap ___ ___
- ☐ Samuel S. Lewis ___ ___
- ☐ Shikellamy ___ ___
- ☐ Susquehanna ___ ___
- ☐ Tuscarora ___ ___
- ☐ Worlds End ___ ___

Counties
- ☐ Berks ___ ___
- ☐ Columbia ___ ___
- ☐ Cumberland ___ ___
- ☐ Dauphin ___ ___
- ☐ Juniata ___ ___
- ☐ Lancaster ___ ___
- ☐ Lebanon ___ ___
- ☐ Luzerne ___ ___
- ☐ Lycoming ___ ___
- ☐ Mifflin ___ ___
- ☐ Montour ___ ___
- ☐ Northumberland ___ ___
- ☐ Perry ___ ___
- ☐ Schuylkill ___ ___
- ☐ Snyder ___ ___
- ☐ Sullivan ___ ___
- ☐ Union ___ ___
- ☐ Wyoming ___ ___
- ☐ York ___ ___

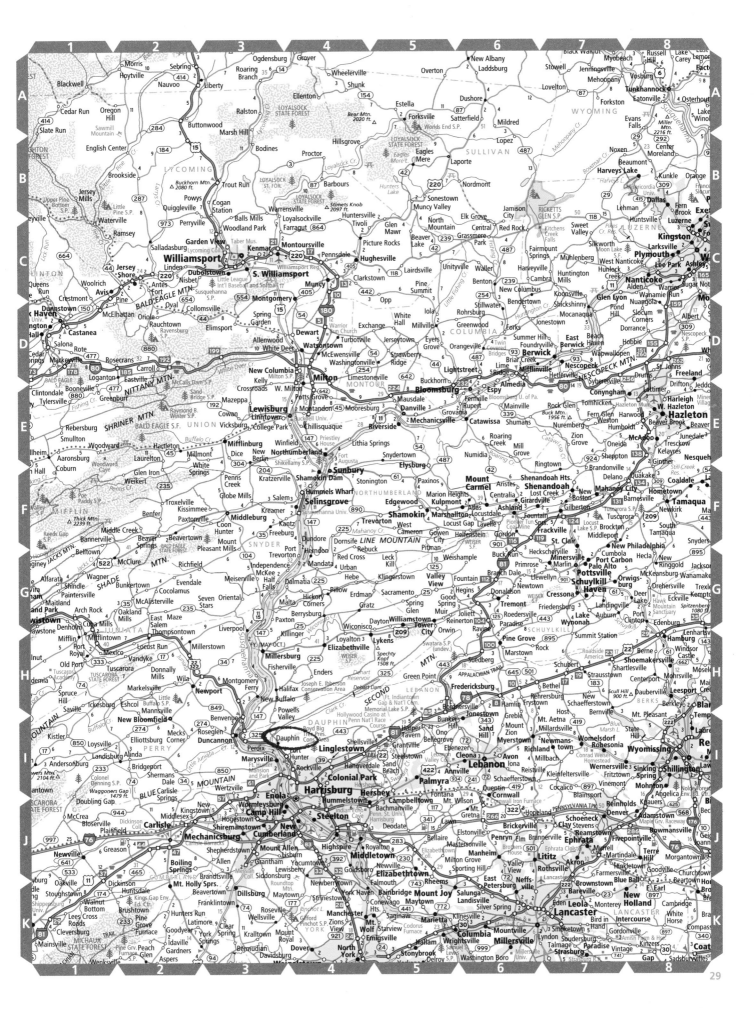

South Carolina
The Palmetto State

Ever seen the movie Edward Scissorhands? There's a garden in Bishopville, SC that makes Scissorhand's creations look bland. Pearl Fryar's Topiary Garden is filled with 300+ sculpted, leafy, non-traditional, awe-inspiring creations. Corkscrew junipers, octopus holly bushes, fish and skeletons shrubs and four-foot letters cut in the yard that proclaim Peace, Love + Goodwill are all born of Fryar's imagination, self-taught skills and his hedge clippers. Grow see for yourself.

How To Map It!™
Use the list below to seek a challenge found on the map and cross it off as you go. **Instructions on page 5.**

Hills & Mills
- ☒ Bishopville D,6
- ☐ Beverly Hills __ __
- ☐ Clarks Hill __ __
- ☐ Cross Hill __ __
- ☐ Fort Mill __ __
- ☐ Holly Hill __ __
- ☐ Honey Hill __ __
- ☐ Inman Mills __ __
- ☐ Liberty Hill __ __
- ☐ Monarch Mill __ __
- ☐ Rock Hill __ __
- ☐ Society Hill __ __
- ☐ Spring Mills __ __
- ☐ Stoney Hill __ __
- ☐ Watts Mills __ __
- ☐ Winnsboro Mills __ __

Creeks & Rivers
- ☐ Ashepoo __ __
- ☐ Black __ __
- ☐ Bush __ __
- ☐ Combahee __ __
- ☐ Congaree __ __
- ☐ Edisto __ __
- ☐ Four Hole __ __
- ☐ Great Pee Dee __ __
- ☐ Long Cane Cr. __ __
- ☐ Lynches __ __
- ☐ N. Fk. Edisto __ __ __
- ☐ Pacolet __ __
- ☐ Santee __ __
- ☐ Savannah __ __
- ☐ Stevens Cr. __ __
- ☐ Tyger __ __
- ☐ Wateree __ __

Lakes
- ☐ Fishing Cr. Res. __ __
- ☐ L. Greenwood __ __
- ☐ L. Marion __ __
- ☐ L. Moultrie __ __
- ☐ L. Murray __ __
- ☐ L. Robinson __ __
- ☐ L. Wylie __ __
- ☐ Monticello Res. __ __
- ☐ Par Pond __ __
- ☐ Wateree L. __ __

Counties
- ☐ Allendale __ __
- ☐ Edgefield __ __
- ☐ Florence __ __
- ☐ Jasper __ __
- ☐ Lexington __ __
- ☐ Marlboro __ __
- ☐ Newberry __ __
- ☐ Williamsburg __ __

Villes
- ☐ Beckhamville __ __
- ☐ Blackville __ __
- ☐ Centerville __ __
- ☐ Dovesville __ __
- ☐ Fingerville __ __
- ☐ Gillisonville __ __
- ☐ Harleyville __ __
- ☐ Hartsville __ __
- ☐ Jenkinsville __ __
- ☐ Mayesville __ __
- ☐ Mountville __ __
- ☐ Parksville __ __
- ☐ Paxville __ __
- ☐ Robertville __ __
- ☐ Rowesville __ __
- ☐ Russellville __ __
- ☐ Tigerville __ __
- ☐ Varnville __ __
- ☐ Woodville __ __

State Parks
- ☐ Aiken S.N.A. __ __
- ☐ Barnwell __ __
- ☐ Cheraw __ __
- ☐ Chester __ __
- ☐ Colleton __ __
- ☐ Croft S.N.A. __ __
- ☐ Dreher I. S.R.A. __ __
- ☐ Edisto Beach __ __
- ☐ Givhans Ferry __ __
- ☐ Hunting Island __ __
- ☐ L. Greenwood S.R.A. __ __
- ☐ Lake Warren __ __
- ☐ Manchester S.F. __ __
- ☐ N.R. Goodale __ __
- ☐ Paris Mtn. __ __
- ☐ Poinsett __ __
- ☐ Sand Hills S.F. __ __
- ☐ Santee __ __

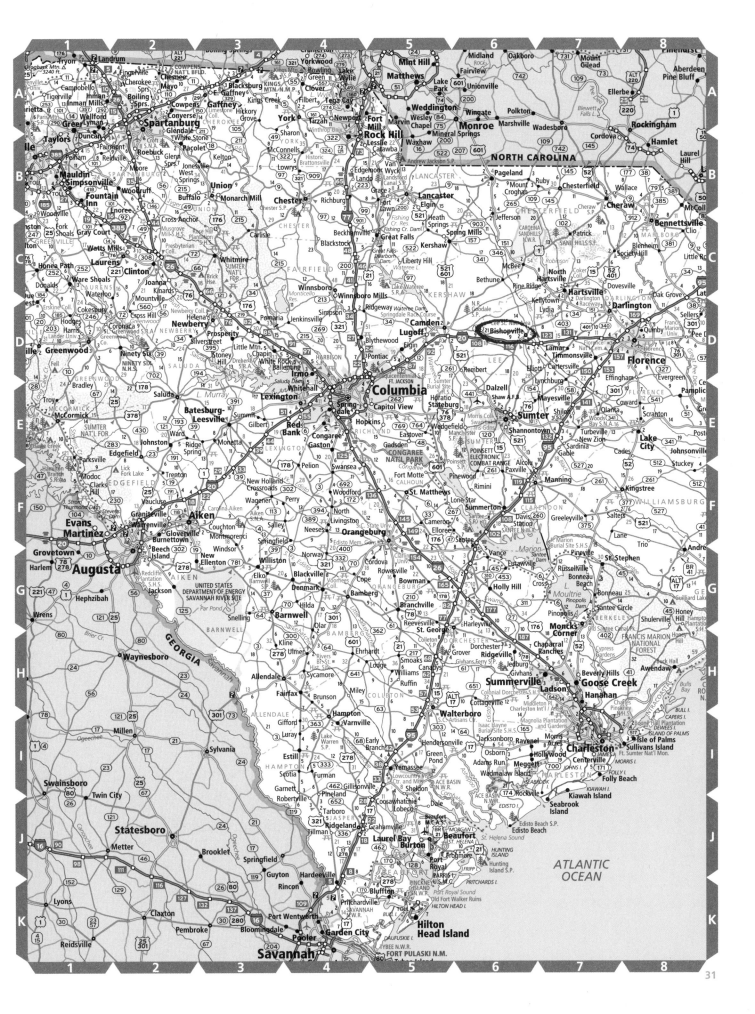

South Dakota
The Mount Rushmore State

Dust off your sunbonnet (my what?) In De Smet, SD you're invited to the Ingalls Homestead where Laura Ingalls, author of the beloved Little House On The Prairie books, lived and wrote and where sunbonnets are encouraged. Go full-pioneer learning in a one-room schoolhouse, driving a covered wagon, making cornhusk dolls, heck they'll even let you do some laundry on a washboard. Your Ma and Pa will be proud.

How To Map It!™

Use the list below to seek a challenge found on the map and cross it off as you go. **Instructions on page 5.**

His Town
- ☒ De Smet E,7
- ❑ Ashton ___
- ❑ Bradley ___
- ❑ Bruce ___
- ❑ Carter ___
- ❑ Chester ___
- ❑ Ellis ___
- ❑ Ethan ___
- ❑ Frederick ___
- ❑ Harrison ___
- ❑ Howard ___
- ❑ Marty ___
- ❑ Marvin ___
- ❑ Parker ___
- ❑ Pierre ___
- ❑ Spencer ___
- ❑ Troy ___
- ❑ Victor ___
- ❑ Virgil ___
- ❑ Wallace ___

Creeks & Rivers
- ❑ Big Sioux ___
- ❑ Choteau Cr. ___
- ❑ Deer ___
- ❑ Dog Ear Cr. ___
- ❑ Elm ___
- ❑ *James ___ , ___
- ❑ Keya Paha ___
- ❑ Little White ___
- ❑ Missouri ___
- ❑ Mud Cr. ___
- ❑ Oak Cr. ___
- ❑ Okobojo Cr. ___
- ❑ Platte Cr. ___
- ❑ Sand Cr. ___
- ❑ Smith Cr. ___
- ❑ Turtle Cr. ___
- ❑ Vermillion ___
- ❑ White Clay ___
- ❑ Wolf Cr. ___

Lakes
- ❑ Bitter L. ___
- ❑ Cottonwood L. ___
- ❑ Elm L. ___
- ❑ L. Bryon ___
- ❑ L. Francis Case ___
- ❑ L. Madison ___
- ❑ L. Whitewood ___
- ❑ Lake Oahe ___
- ❑ Mud L. Res. ___
- ❑ Platte L. ___
- ❑ Red L. ___
- ❑ Richmond L. ___
- ❑ Salt L. ___
- ❑ Spring L. ___
- ❑ Stone L. ___
- ❑ Swan L. ___
- ❑ Waubay L. ___
- ❑ White L. ___

Her Town
- ❑ Astoria ___
- ❑ Aurora ___
- ❑ Avon ___
- ❑ Chelsea ___
- ❑ Eden ___
- ❑ Emery ___
- ❑ Florence ___
- ❑ Hazel ___
- ❑ Kaylor ___
- ❑ Leola ___
- ❑ Lily ___
- ❑ Mina ___
- ❑ Onida ___
- ❑ Ravinia ___
- ❑ Romona ___
- ❑ Rosebud ___
- ❑ Roslyn ___

State Parks
- ❑ Buryanek S.R.A. ___
- ❑ Fisher Grv. ___
- ❑ Indian Cr. S.R.A. ___
- ❑ Lake Louise S.R.A. ___
- ❑ Lake Poinsett S.R.A. ___
- ❑ Lake Vermillion S.R.A. ___
- ❑ Little Moreau S.R.A. ___
- ❑ Mina Lake S.R.A. ___
- ❑ Newton Hills ___
- ❑ Oakwood Lakes ___
- ❑ Okobojo Pt. S.R.A. ___
- ❑ Pease Cr. S.R.A. ___
- ❑ Pelican Lake S.R.A. ___
- ❑ Roy Lake ___
- ❑ Sica Hollow ___
- ❑ Springfield S.R.A. ___
- ❑ Union Grove ___
- ❑ W. Bend S.R.A. ___

* Multiple coordinates | Puzzle solutions pages 54-64

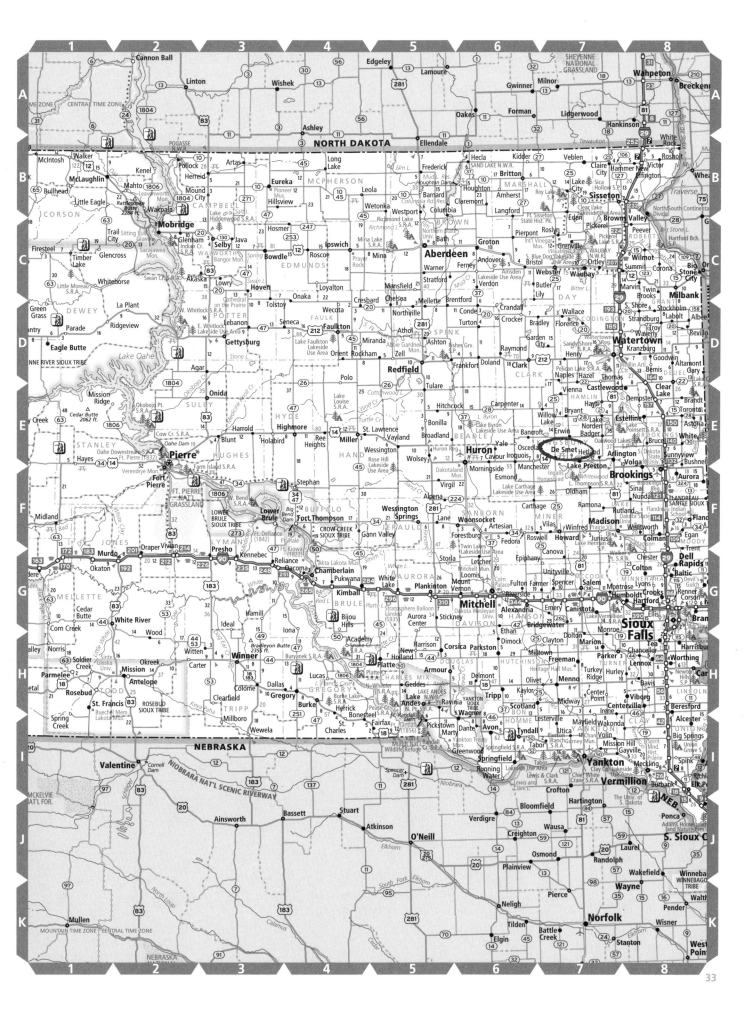

Tennessee
The Volunteer State

Many dream of cutting a record in Nashville, TN. Dreams come true at Third Man Records on 7th Ave South, where you can step into refurbished 1947 Voice-o-Graph Record Booth to record about 150 seconds of audio onto a six-inch phonograph disc. For $20 people have stepped in to record songs, marriage proposals, one-act plays, wills and jokes. Even a few recording stars have taken it for a spin. You could be a hit!

How To Map It!™

Use the list below to seek a challenge found on the map and cross it off as you go. **Instructions on page 5.**

Towns
- ☒ Nashville D,5
- ☐ Alto __ __
- ☐ Bible Hill __ __
- ☐ Burnt Church __ __
- ☐ Cash Point __ __
- ☐ Chapel Hill __ __
- ☐ Cuba Landing __ __
- ☐ Difficult __ __
- ☐ Flatwoods __ __
- ☐ Fly __ __
- ☐ Fountain Head __ __
- ☐ Iron City __ __
- ☐ Mount Joy __ __
- ☐ New Deal __ __
- ☐ New Union __ __
- ☐ Only __ __
- ☐ Pleasant View __ __
- ☐ Rome __ __
- ☐ *Shiloh __ __ , __ __
- ☐ Sugar Tree __ __
- ☐ White House __ __

Rivers
- ☐ Big Sandy __ __
- ☐ Buffalo __ __
- ☐ Cumberland __ __
- ☐ *Duck __ __ , __ __
- ☐ E. Fk. Stones __ __
- ☐ Elk __ __
- ☐ Harpeth __ __
- ☐ Piney __ __
- ☐ Shoal __ __
- ☐ *Tennessee __ __ ,

Lakes
- ☐ J. Percy Priest L. __ __
- ☐ L. Barkley __ __
- ☐ Normandy Lake __ __
- ☐ Old Hickory L. __ __
- ☐ Tims Ford L. __ __
- ☐ Woods Res. __ __

State Parks
- ☐ Bledsoe Cr. __ __
- ☐ Cedars of Lebanon __ __
- ☐ David Crockett __ __
- ☐ Dunbar Cave __ __
- ☐ Edgar Evins __ __
- ☐ Harpeth River __ __
- ☐ Henry Horton __ __
- ☐ Johnsonville __ __
- ☐ Lewis __ __
- ☐ Long Hunter __ __
- ☐ Montgomery Bell __ __
- ☐ Nathan Bedford Forrest __ __
- ☐ Paris Landing __ __
- ☐ Pickwick Landing __ __
- ☐ Port Royal __ __
- ☐ Stewart __ __
- ☐ Tims Ford __ __

Villes
- ☐ Almaville __ __
- ☐ Belleville __ __
- ☐ Campbellsville __ __
- ☐ Centerville __ __
- ☐ Decaturville __ __
- ☐ Eagleville __ __
- ☐ Fayetteville __ __
- ☐ Gladeville __ __
- ☐ Hartsville __ __
- ☐ Henryville __ __
- ☐ Johnsonville __ __
- ☐ Leeville __ __
- ☐ Lobelville __ __
- ☐ Manlyville __ __
- ☐ Mitchellville __ __
- ☐ Nolensville __ __
- ☐ Perryville __ __
- ☐ Readyville __ __
- ☐ Springville __ __
- ☐ Summitville __ __
- ☐ Unionville __ __

Counties
- ☐ Benton __ __
- ☐ Coffee __ __
- ☐ Decatur __ __
- ☐ Dickson __ __
- ☐ Franklin __ __
- ☐ Giles __ __
- ☐ Hardin __ __
- ☐ Hickman __ __
- ☐ Houston __ __
- ☐ Lincoln __ __
- ☐ Marshall __ __
- ☐ Moore __ __
- ☐ Perry __ __
- ☐ Robertson __ __
- ☐ Rutherford __ __
- ☐ Stewart __ __
- ☐ Sumner __ __
- ☐ Trousdale __ __
- ☐ Wayne __ __
- ☐ Wilson __ __

* Multiple coordinates | Puzzle solutions pages 54-64

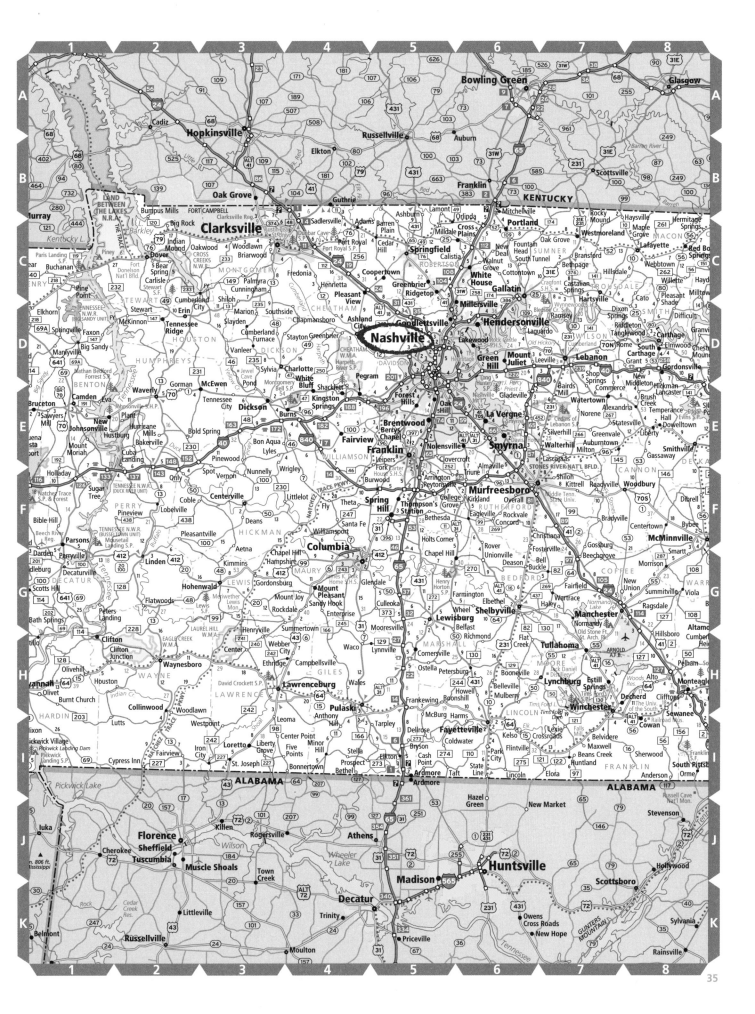

Texas
The Lone Star State

It's true. Everything's bigger in Texas. Like the Big Red Button (BRB). The one you push to cause The Big Bubble to erupt in the Buffalo Bayou waters under Houston's Preston Street Bridge. Tucked into one of the bridge pillars, the BRB is soooo tempting – by design. Installed in 1998, the big button doubles as art and infrastructure by triggering curiosity as well as a blast of oxygen to bubble the stagnant water. Big fun! (Try not to startle the kayakers.)

How To Map It!™

Use the list below to seek a challenge found on the map and cross it off as you go. **Instructions on page 5.**

Hills & Springs
- ☒ Houston **I,6**
- ❏ Chappell Hill _ _
- ❏ Dalby Springs _ _
- ❏ Dripping Springs _ _
- ❏ Forest Hill _ _
- ❏ Gay Hill _ _
- ❏ High Hill _ _
- ❏ Laird Hill _ _
- ❏ Liberty Hill _ _
- ❏ Moss Hill _ _
- ❏ Myrtle Springs _ _
- ❏ Park Springs _ _
- ❏ Payne Springs _ _
- ❏ Prairie Hill _ _
- ❏ Rek Hill _ _
- ❏ Rolling Hills _ _
- ❏ Sutherland Springs _ _
- ❏ The Hills _ _
- ❏ Thorp Spring _ _

Rivers
- ❏ Blanco _ _
- ❏ *Brazos _ _ , _ _
- ❏ Leon _ _
- ❏ Little _ _
- ❏ N. Bosque _ _
- ❏ Navasota _ _
- ❏ Neches _ _
- ❏ *Trinity _ _ , _ _

Lakes
- ❏ Cedar Cr. Res. _ _
- ❏ Fairfield L. _ _
- ❏ L. Bridgeport _ _
- ❏ L. Conroe _ _
- ❏ L. Limestone _ _
- ❏ L. Livingston _ _
- ❏ L. Palestine _ _
- ❏ L. Tawakoni _ _
- ❏ Lake O' The Pines _ _

State Parks
- ❏ Bastrop _ _
- ❏ Brazos Bend _ _
- ❏ Buescher _ _
- ❏ Cleburne _ _
- ❏ Daingerfield _ _
- ❏ Dinosaur Valley _ _
- ❏ Fairfield Lake _ _
- ❏ Ft. Parker _ _
- ❏ Galveston Island _ _
- ❏ Huntsville _ _
- ❏ Lake Tawakoni _ _
- ❏ Lake Whitney _ _
- ❏ Lockhart _ _
- ❏ Martin Cr. Lake _ _
- ❏ Meridian _ _
- ❏ Mission Tejas _ _
- ❏ Mother Neff _ _
- ❏ Palmetto _ _
- ❏ Purtis Cr. _ _
- ❏ Tyler _ _

Villes
- ❏ Ammannsville _ _ _
- ❏ Bruceville-Eddy _ _
- ❏ Centerville _ _
- ❏ Cookville _ _
- ❏ Deanville _ _
- ❏ Farmersville _ _
- ❏ Gatesville _ _
- ❏ Hallsville _ _
- ❏ Huntsville _ _
- ❏ Jacksonville _ _
- ❏ Laneville _ _
- ❏ Madisonville _ _
- ❏ Needville _ _
- ❏ Nolanville _ _
- ❏ Poolville _ _
- ❏ Prairieville _ _
- ❏ Rutersville _ _
- ❏ Smithville _ _
- ❏ Somerville _ _
- ❏ Turnersville _ _

Counties
- ❏ Anderson _ _
- ❏ Burnet _ _
- ❏ Colorado _ _
- ❏ Denton _ _
- ❏ Erath _ _
- ❏ Falls _ _
- ❏ Guadalupe _ _
- ❏ Hill _ _
- ❏ Hood _ _
- ❏ Jack _ _
- ❏ Leon _ _
- ❏ Montgomery _ _
- ❏ Navarro _ _
- ❏ Parker _ _
- ❏ Robertson _ _
- ❏ San Jacinto _ _
- ❏ Trinity _ _
- ❏ Van Zandt _ _
- ❏ Walker _ _
- ❏ Waller _ _

* Multiple coordinates | Puzzle solutions pages 54-64

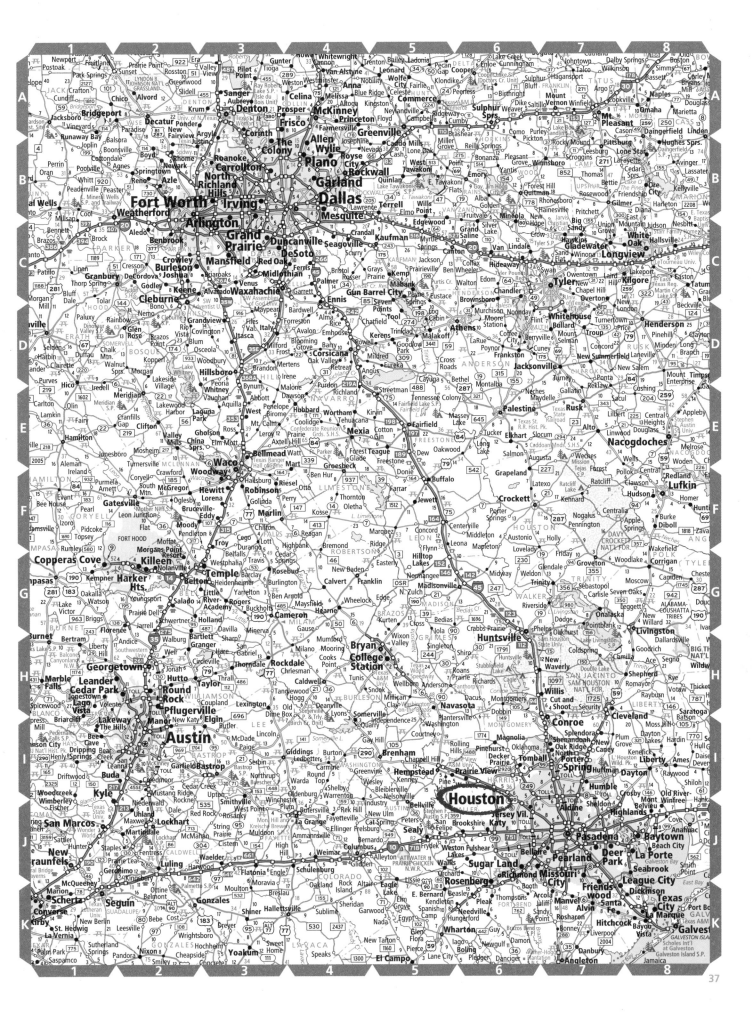

Utah
The Beehive State

Don't judge a book by its crater. Wait. Make that a crater by its cover. Like the 55-foot hill in Midway, Utah that covers the magical Homestead Crater. This geothermal spring, over 10,000 years old, is a nature-made hot tub. It's heated by the earth's interior two miles below the surface and it's so big that you can soak, swim, snorkel, scuba or paddleboard yoga in its gorgeous 90 degree mineral water. Ahhhh.

How To Map It!™
Use the list below to seek a challenge found on the map and cross it off as you go. **Instructions on page 5.**

Towns
- ☒ Midway B,3
- ❏ Antimony __ __
- ❏ Birdseye __ __
- ❏ Bluebell __ __
- ❏ Bullfrog __ __
- ❏ Devils Slide __ __
- ❏ Dry Fork __ __
- ❏ Dutch John __ __
- ❏ Echo __ __
- ❏ Elmo __ __
- ❏ Fountain Green __ __
- ❏ Fruitland __ __
- ❏ Helper __ __
- ❏ Hideout __ __
- ❏ Independence __ __
- ❏ Kenilworth __ __
- ❏ Meadow __ __
- ❏ Rush Valley __ __
- ❏ Sunnyside __ __
- ❏ Wales __ __

Creeks & Rivers
- ❏ Big Brush __ __
- ❏ Bitter Cr. __ __
- ❏ Cottonwood Cr. __ __
- ❏ Dirty Devil __ __
- ❏ Duchesne __ __
- ❏ E. Fk. Sevier __ __
- ❏ Escalante __ __
- ❏ *Green __ __
- ❏ Hatch Wash __ __
- ❏ Lake Fk. __ __
- ❏ Muddy Cr. __ __
- ❏ Nine Mile Cr. __ __
- ❏ Otter Cr. __ __
- ❏ Price __ __
- ❏ Provo __ __
- ❏ Rock Cr. __ __
- ❏ San Rafael __ __
- ❏ Sevier __ __
- ❏ Whiterocks __ __
- ❏ Willow Cr. __ __

Mountains & Peaks
- ❏ Cedar Mtn. __ __
- ❏ Delano Peak __ __
- ❏ Gilbert Peak __ __
- ❏ Hilgard Mtn. __ __
- ❏ Indian Head Peak __ __
- ❏ Mt. Agassiz __ __
- ❏ Mt. Belknap __ __
- ❏ Mt. Catherine __ __
- ❏ Mt. Dutton __ __
- ❏ Mt. Ellen __ __
- ❏ Mt. Lena __ __
- ❏ Mt. Linnaeus __ __
- ❏ Mt. Nebo __ __
- ❏ N. Sixshooter Peak __ __
- ❏ Shay Mtn. __ __
- ❏ Temple Mtn. __ __
- ❏ Tintic Mtn. __ __
- ❏ Window Blind Peak __ __

State Parks
- ❏ Antelope Island __ __
- ❏ Dead Horse Pt. __ __
- ❏ Deer Cr. __ __
- ❏ E. Canyon __ __
- ❏ Goblin Valley __ __
- ❏ Green River __ __
- ❏ Huntington __ __
- ❏ Jordanelle __ __
- ❏ Kodachrome Basin __ __
- ❏ Millsite __ __
- ❏ Palisade __ __
- ❏ Piute __ __
- ❏ Rockport __ __
- ❏ Scofield __ __
- ❏ Steinaker __ __
- ❏ Utah Lake __ __
- ❏ Wasatch Mtn. __ __
- ❏ Yuba __ __

Lakes
- ❏ Bottle Hollow Res. __ __
- ❏ Clear L. __ __
- ❏ DMAD Res. __ __
- ❏ Fish L. __ __
- ❏ Gunnison Res. __ __
- ❏ Joes Valley Res. __ __
- ❏ Mona Res. __ __
- ❏ Moon L. __ __
- ❏ Oaks Park Res. __ __
- ❏ Otter Cr. Res. __ __
- ❏ Pelican L. __ __
- ❏ Piute Res. __ __
- ❏ Rockport L. __ __
- ❏ Scofield Res. __ __
- ❏ Starvation Res. __ __
- ❏ Steinaker Res. __ __
- ❏ Strawberry Res. __ __
- ❏ Utah Lake __ __

* Multiple coordinates | Puzzle solutions pages 54-64

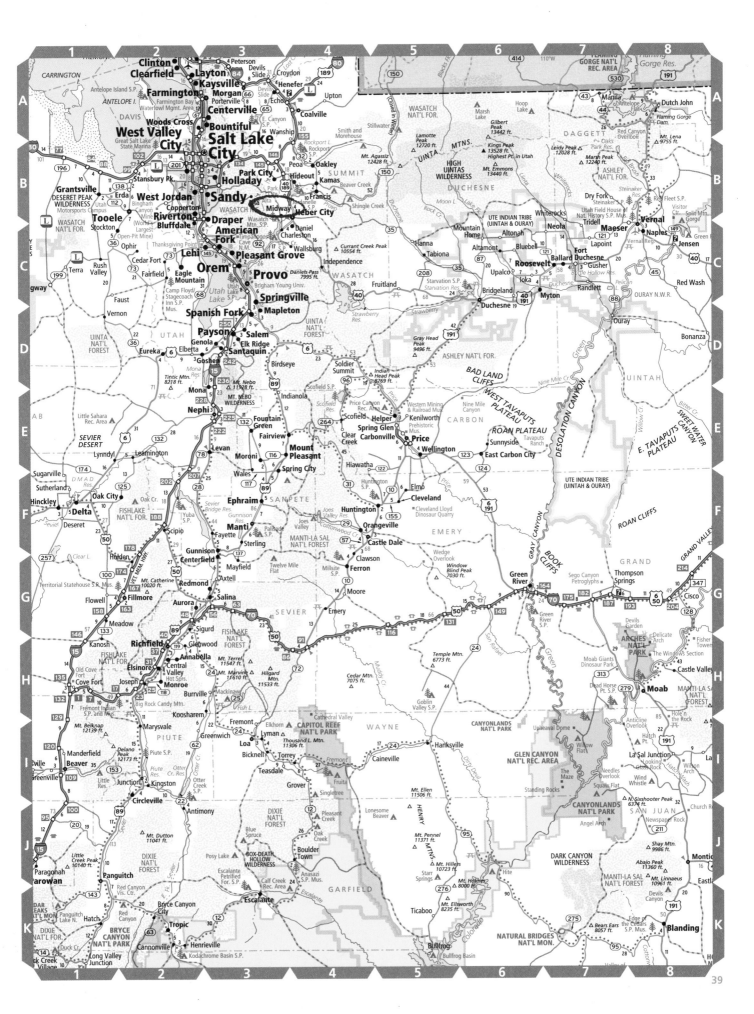

Vermont
The Green Mountain State

If you're in Stowe, VT the hills are truly alive, because here is where the *Sound of Music* von Trapp family has been welcoming visitors to their Trapp Family Lodge since 1950. After fleeing Austria, the family moved to this 2,400-acre estate with mountain top views reminiscent of their homeland. Take a tour and learn about their history, enjoy their farm, ski, hike, and visit their bierhall for a von Trapp lager…that'll get you singing!

How To Map It! ™
Use the list below to seek a challenge found on the map and cross it off as you go. **Instructions on page 5.**

Villes
- ☒ Stowe D,4
- ❏ Beanville __ __
- ❏ Blissville __ __
- ❏ Cookville __ __
- ❏ Cuttingsville __ __
- ❏ Danville __ __
- ❏ Felchville __ __
- ❏ Gaysville __ __
- ❏ Granville __ __
- ❏ Healdville __ __
- ❏ Hectorville __ __
- ❏ Irasville __ __
- ❏ Jeffersonville __ __
- ❏ Jonesville __ __
- ❏ Lyndonville __ __
- ❏ Proctorsville __ __
- ❏ Putnanville __ __
- ❏ Taftsville __ __
- ❏ Tarbellville __ __
- ❏ Waterville __ __
- ❏ Websterville __ __

Creeks & Rivers
- ❏ Black Br __ __,
- ❏ Clyde __ __
- ❏ Joes __ __
- ❏ La Platte __ __
- ❏ Lamoille __ __
- ❏ Lemon Fair __ __
- ❏ Mad __ __
- ❏ Mettawee __ __
- ❏ Mill __ __
- ❏ Moose __ __
- ❏ Nulhegan __ __
- ❏ Paul __ __
- ❏ Third Br. __ __
- ❏ Waits __ __
- ❏ Wells __ __
- ❏ *White __ __,
  __ __
- ❏ Winooski __ __

Mountains & Peaks
- ❏ Bloodroot Mtn. __ __
- ❏ Bread Loaf Mtn. __ __
- ❏ Burke Mtn. __ __
- ❏ Gile Mtn. __ __
- ❏ Gore Mtn. __ __
- ❏ Granby Mtn. __ __
- ❏ Harris Mtn. __ __
- ❏ Jay Peak __ __
- ❏ Killington Pk. __ __
- ❏ Ludlow Mtn. __ __
- ❏ Monadnock Mtn. __ __
- ❏ Mt. Grant __ __
- ❏ Mt. Hunger __ __
- ❏ Mt. John __ __
- ❏ Sable Mtn. __ __
- ❏ Snake Mtn. __ __
- ❏ Stannard Mtn. __ __
- ❏ Stone Mtn. __ __
- ❏ Tinmouth Mtn. __ __
- ❏ White Face Mtn. __ __

Lakes
- ❏ Arrowhead Mtn. L. __ __
- ❏ Caspian L. __ __
- ❏ Echo L. __ __
- ❏ Great Averill Pd. __ __
- ❏ Great Hosmer Pd. __ __
- ❏ Hardwick L. __ __
- ❏ Island Pd. __ __
- ❏ L. Bomoseen __ __
- ❏ L. Carmi __ __
- ❏ L. Dunmore __ __
- ❏ L. Fairlee __ __
- ❏ L. Groton __ __
- ❏ L. Iroquois __ __
- ❏ *Lake Champlain
- ❏ Little Averill L. __ __
- ❏ Maidstone L. __ __
- ❏ Norton Pd. __ __
- ❏ Waterbury Res. __ __
- ❏ Wrightsville Res. __ __

Ski
- ❏ Bolton Valley __ __
- ❏ Jay Peak __ __
- ❏ Killington __ __
- ❏ Mad River Glen __ __
- ❏ Middlebury Coll. Snow Bowl __ __
- ❏ Okemo Mtn. __ __
- ❏ Pico Mtn. __ __
- ❏ Q Burke Mtn. __ __
- ❏ Smugglers' Notch __ __
- ❏ Stowe Mtn. __ __
- ❏ Sugarbush __ __
- ❏ Suicide Six __ __

State Parks
- ❏ Allis __ __
- ❏ Brighton __ __
- ❏ Half Moon Pd. __ __
- ❏ Kill Kare __ __
- ❏ Maidstone __ __
- ❏ Smugglers Notch __ __

* Multiple coordinates | Puzzle solutions pages 54-64

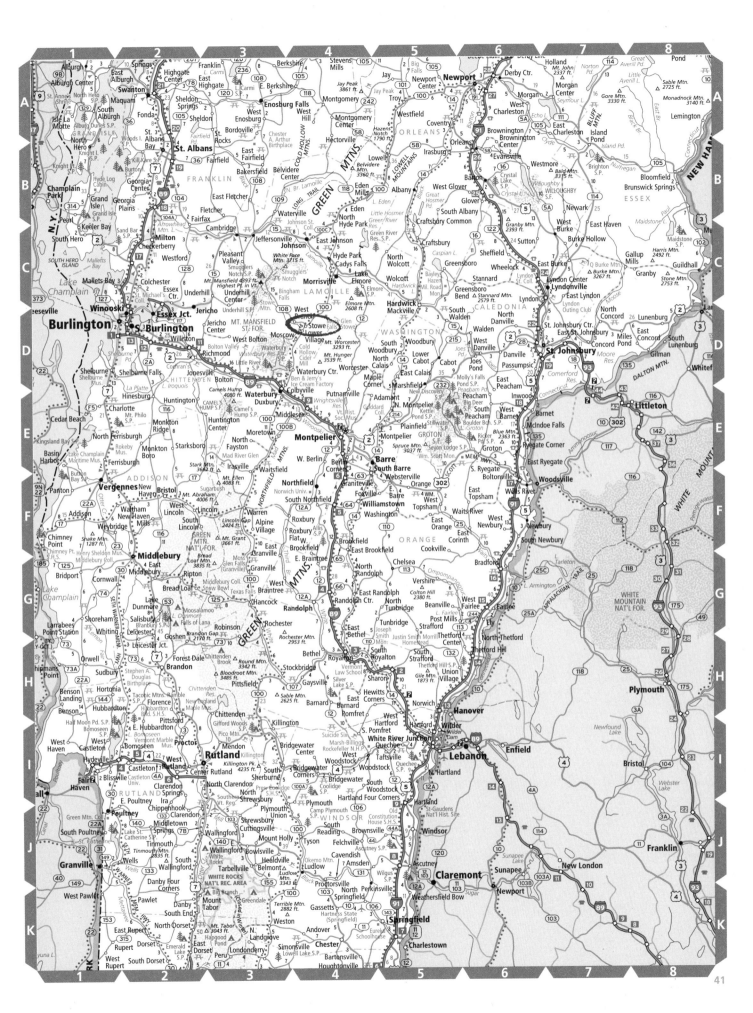

Virginia
Old Dominion

Sometimes it rains on your parade. But, if you're at American Celebration On Parade in Shenandoah Caverns, VA, let it rain. You'll be dry inside a gigantic warehouse packed with old floats from Presidential Inaugurals, the Rose Parade, Miss America Parade, Thanksgiving parades and many more. Walk past a 30-foot genie, a banjo playing pelican, an Iwo Jima Memorial, King Tut, astronauts and lots more glittery, mammoth, kind of spooky American parade-ery all under one roof.

How To Map It!™
Use the list below to seek a challenge found on the map and cross it off as you go. **Instructions on page 5.**

Towns
- ☒ Shenandoah Caverns B,3
- ☐ Alma __
- ☐ Boston __ __
- ☐ Bumpass __
- ☐ Cootes Store __ __
- ☐ Dinwiddie __ __
- ☐ Free Union __ __
- ☐ Goochland __ __
- ☐ Madison __ __
- ☐ Moscow __ __
- ☐ Nutbush __ __
- ☐ Paris __ __
- ☐ Red House __ __
- ☐ Sunny Side __ __
- ☐ Tenth Legion __ __
- ☐ Victoria __ __
- ☐ Vienna __ __
- ☐ Washington __ __
- ☐ Yale __ __

Hills & Mounts
- ☐ Burr Hill __ __
- ☐ Clover Hill __ __
- ☐ Crystal Hill __ __
- ☐ Fishers Hill __ __
- ☐ Flint Hill __ __
- ☐ Independent Hill __ __
- ☐ Mount Airy __ __
- ☐ Mount Clifton __ __
- ☐ Mount Crawford __ __
- ☐ Mount Laurel __ __
- ☐ Mount Olive __ __
- ☐ Mount Sidney __ __
- ☐ Mount Solon __ __
- ☐ Oak Hill __ __
- ☐ South Hill __ __
- ☐ Vernon Hill __ __

State Parks
- ☐ Bear Cr. Lake __ __
- ☐ Celedon Nat. Area __ __
- ☐ Cumberland __ __
- ☐ Holliday Lake __ __
- ☐ James River __ __
- ☐ Lake Anna __ __
- ☐ Leesylvania __ __
- ☐ Mason Neck __ __
- ☐ Pocahontas __ __
- ☐ Prince William For. Pk. __ __
- ☐ Sailor's Cr. Bfld. H.S.P. __ __
- ☐ Shenandoah R. "Andy Guest" __ __
- ☐ Sky Meadows __ __
- ☐ Staunton River Bfld. __ __
- ☐ Twin Lakes __ __
- ☐ Zoar S.F. __ __

Villes
- ☐ Bentonville __ __
- ☐ Cedarville __ __
- ☐ Clayville __ __
- ☐ Covesville __ __
- ☐ Craigsville __ __
- ☐ Deatonville __ __
- ☐ Farmville __ __
- ☐ Gordonsville __ __
- ☐ Greenville __ __
- ☐ Hadensville __ __
- ☐ Jetersville __ __
- ☐ Lawrenceville __ __
- ☐ Lowesville __ __
- ☐ Madisonville __ __
- ☐ Nortonsville __ __
- ☐ Roseville __ __
- ☐ Sperryville __ __
- ☐ Timberville __ __
- ☐ Upperville __ __

Counties
- ☐ Amelia __ __
- ☐ Augusta __ __
- ☐ Brunswick __ __
- ☐ Campbell __ __
- ☐ Caroline __ __
- ☐ Dinwiddie __ __
- ☐ Goochland __ __
- ☐ Greensville __ __
- ☐ Hanover __ __
- ☐ Henrico __ __
- ☐ King George __ __
- ☐ Madison __ __
- ☐ Nottoway __ __
- ☐ Orange __ __
- ☐ Prince Edward __ __
- ☐ Prince William __ __
- ☐ Stafford __ __
- ☐ Sussex __ __
- ☐ Warren __ __

Puzzle solutions pages 54-64

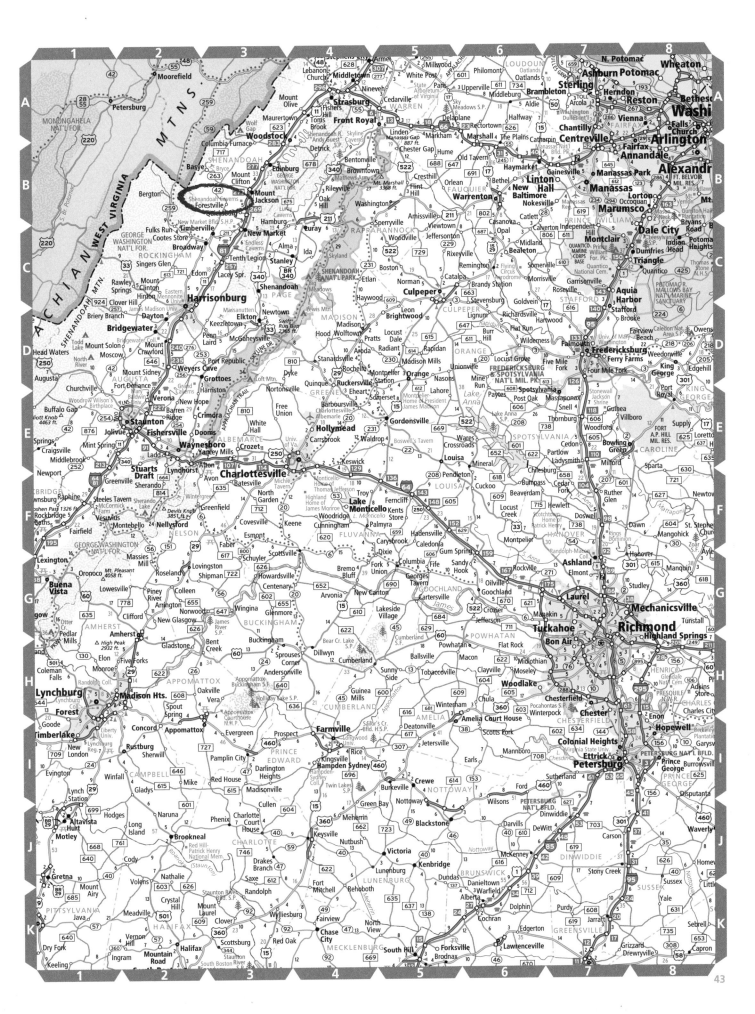

Washington
The Evergreen State

Who goes there? *Pffft,* typical troll question, right? But, if you answer "me" then you're probably standing on the Aurora Bridge in the Seattle, WA Fremont neighborhood. And the Fremont Troll is right underneath you. Go see. He's been haunting the place since 1990. He's 18-feet tall, he's gripping an old VW in his hand, its hubcap is in his eye and he doesn't care if you climb on him (no one's been gobbled up…yet.)

How To Map It!™

Use the list below to seek a challenge found on the map and cross it off as you go. **Instructions on page 5.**

Towns	Creeks & Rivers	Lakes	Peaks & Mountains	State Parks
☒ Seattle E,6	☐ Black __ __	☐ Alder L. __ __	☐ Boistfort Peak __ __	☐ Anderson Lake __ __
☐ Alder __ __	☐ Carbon __ __	☐ Baker L. __ __	☐ Elk Mtn. __ __	☐ Birch Bay __ __
☐ Beaver __ __	☐ Cowlitz __ __	☐ Black L. __ __	☐ Ellis Mtn. __ __	☐ Deception Pass __ __
☐ Concrete __ __	☐ Dickey __ __	☐ Chester Morse L. __ __	☐ Gee Pt. __ __	☐ Flaming Geyser __ __
☐ Deer Harbor __ __	☐ Dungeness __ __	☐ Dickey L. __ __	☐ Griffin Mtn. __ __	☐ Ft. Ebey __ __
☐ Forks __ __	☐ Elwha __ __	☐ L. Cavanaugh __ __	☐ Haystack Mtn. __ __	☐ Illahee __ __
☐ Gold Bar __ __	☐ Grays __ __	☐ L. Crescent __ __	☐ Kiona Pk. __ __	☐ Jones Island __ __
☐ Lilliwaup __ __	☐ Green __ __	☐ L. Quinault __ __	☐ Mt. Anderson __ __	☐ Lewis and Clark __ __
☐ Maple Falls __ __	☐ Hoh __ __	☐ L. Roesiger __ __	☐ Mt. Baker __ __	☐ Matia Island __ __
☐ Maytown __ __	☐ N. Fk. Nooksack __ __	☐ L. Shannon __ __	☐ Mt. Carrie __ __	☐ Mystery Bay __ __
☐ Nahcotta __ __	☐ Nisqually __ __	☐ L. Tapps __ __	☐ Mt. Constance __ __	☐ Nolte __ __
☐ Orcas __ __	☐ Pilchuck Cr. __ __	☐ L. Whatcom __ __	☐ Mt. Deception __ __	☐ Olallie __ __
☐ Poulsbo __ __	☐ Puyallup __ __	☐ Lake Sammamish __ __	☐ Mt. Higgins __ __	☐ Patos Island __ __
☐ Queets __ __	☐ Quinault __ __	☐ Mason L. __ __	☐ Mt. Stickney __ __	☐ Rainbow Falls __ __
☐ Robe __ __	☐ Satsop __ __	☐ Mayfield L. __ __	☐ S. Twin __ __	☐ Rasar __ __
☐ Tokeland __ __	☐ Skookumchuck __ __	☐ Packwood L. __ __	☐ Storm King Mtn. __ __	☐ Shine Tidelands __ __
☐ Union __ __	☐ Snoqualmie __ __	☐ Riffe Lake __ __	☐ The Brothers __ __	☐ Spencer Spit __ __
☐ Vader __ __	☐ Willapa __ __	☐ Summit L. __ __	☐ Three Fingers __ __	☐ Twin Harbors __ __
☐ Warm Beach __ __	☐ Wynoochee __ __	☐ Wynoochee L. __ __	☐ Walville Pk. __ __	☐ Wenberg __ __

Puzzle solutions pages 54-64

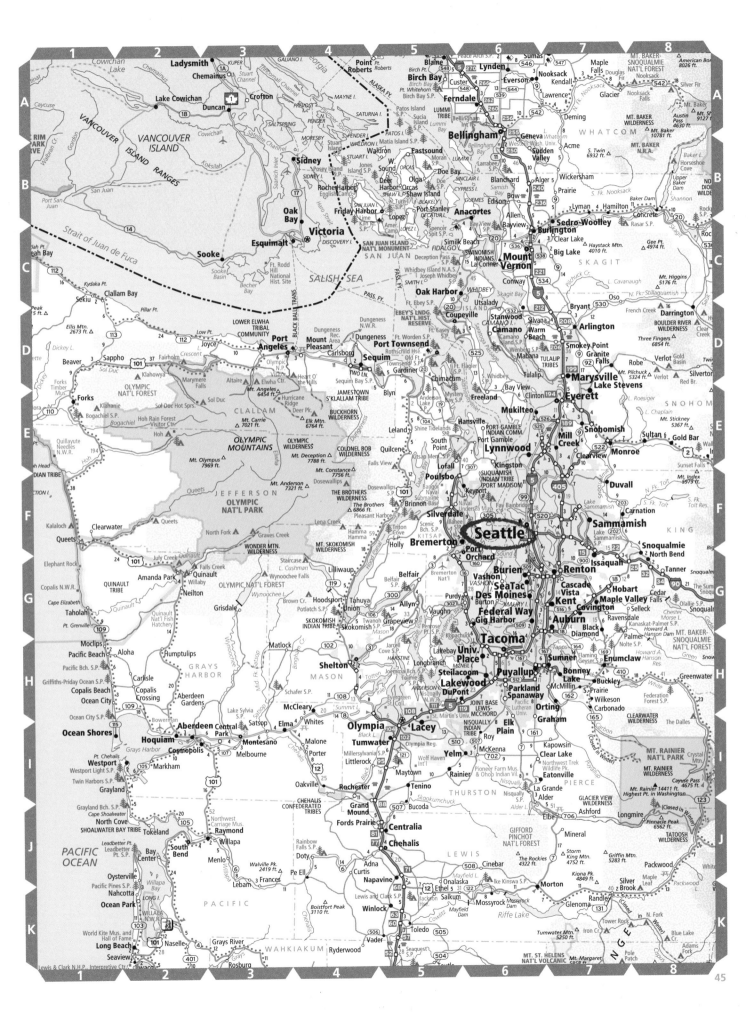

Washington, D.C.
Capital of the United States

Capitol or capital? It's both at D.C.'s Rock Creek Park where someone thought that discarding stones from the U.S. Capitol Building was a capital idea. Sounds crazy but the "Capitol stones" are actual marble and sandstone pieces from the building, torn off during a 1958 renovation and then stacked up behind a park maintenance shed. Now mossy and settled in, this unmarked and unofficial, historic monument is capital for being so Capitol.

How To Map It!™

Use the list below to seek a challenge found on the map and cross it off as you go. **Instructions on page 5.**

Towns

- ☒ Rock Creek Park E,5
- ❑ Ashton ___
- ❑ Belvedere ___
- ❑ Chapel Acres ___
- ❑ Defense Hts. ___
- ❑ Emory Grove ___
- ❑ Four Corners ___
- ❑ Friendly ___
- ❑ Good Hope ___
- ❑ Hillcrest Heights ___
- ❑ Jefferson Vil. ___
- ❑ Kings Park ___
- ❑ Leisure World ___
- ❑ N. Chevy Chase ___
- ❑ Old Farm ___
- ❑ Quince Orchard ___
- ❑ Seven Corners ___
- ❑ Shady Oak ___
- ❑ Wellington ___

Blvds. & Roads

- ❑ Aspen Hill Rd. ___
- ❑ Backlick Rd. ___
- ❑ Dolly Madison Blvd. ___
- ❑ Foxhall Rd. ___
- ❑ Good Hope Rd. ___
- ❑ Hooes Rd. ___
- ❑ Kenilworth Ave. ___
- ❑ Long Draft Rd. ___
- ❑ Marlboro Pike ___
- ❑ *Military Rd. ___, ___
- ❑ Needwood Rd. ___
- ❑ *Pennsylvania Ave. ___, ___
- ❑ Sherriff Rd. ___
- ❑ Sleepy Hollow Rd. ___
- ❑ Turkey Foot Rd. ___
- ❑ Van Dusen Rd. ___

Creeks & Rivers

- ❑ Accotink ___
- ❑ Anacostia ___
- ❑ Beaverdam ___
- ❑ Cabin John ___
- ❑ Difficult Run ___
- ❑ Henson ___
- ❑ Little Hunting ___
- ❑ Northwest Branch ___
- ❑ Pohick ___
- ❑ Potomac ___
- ❑ Rock ___
- ❑ Tinkers ___

Lakes

- ❑ Dalecarlia Res. ___
- ❑ Greenbelt Lake ___
- ❑ L. Barcroft ___
- ❑ L. Nirvana ___
- ❑ L. Placid ___
- ❑ McMillan Res. ___

Golf Courses

- ❑ *Army Navy ___, ___
- ❑ Avenel ___
- ❑ Bethesda ___
- ❑ Burning Tree ___
- ❑ Chevy Chase ___
- ❑ Columbia ___
- ❑ Congressional ___
- ❑ Falls Road ___
- ❑ Golf Course ___
- ❑ Greendale ___
- ❑ Gunpowder ___
- ❑ Kenwood ___
- ❑ Langston ___
- ❑ Manor ___
- ❑ Needwood ___
- ❑ Norbeck ___
- ❑ Pinecrest ___
- ❑ Springfield ___
- ❑ Trotters Glen ___

Hills & Villes

- ❑ Aspen Hill ___
- ❑ Beltsville ___
- ❑ Burtonsville ___
- ❑ Coral Hills ___
- ❑ Glen Hills ___
- ❑ Hyattsville ___
- ❑ Landover Hills ___
- ❑ Lewinsville ___
- ❑ Masonville ___
- ❑ Oxon Hill ___
- ❑ Pimmit Hills ___
- ❑ Randolph Hills ___
- ❑ Scaggsville ___
- ❑ Silver Hill ___
- ❑ Spencerville ___
- ❑ Temple Hill ___
- ❑ Virginia Hills ___

* Multiple coordinates | Puzzle solutions pages 54-64

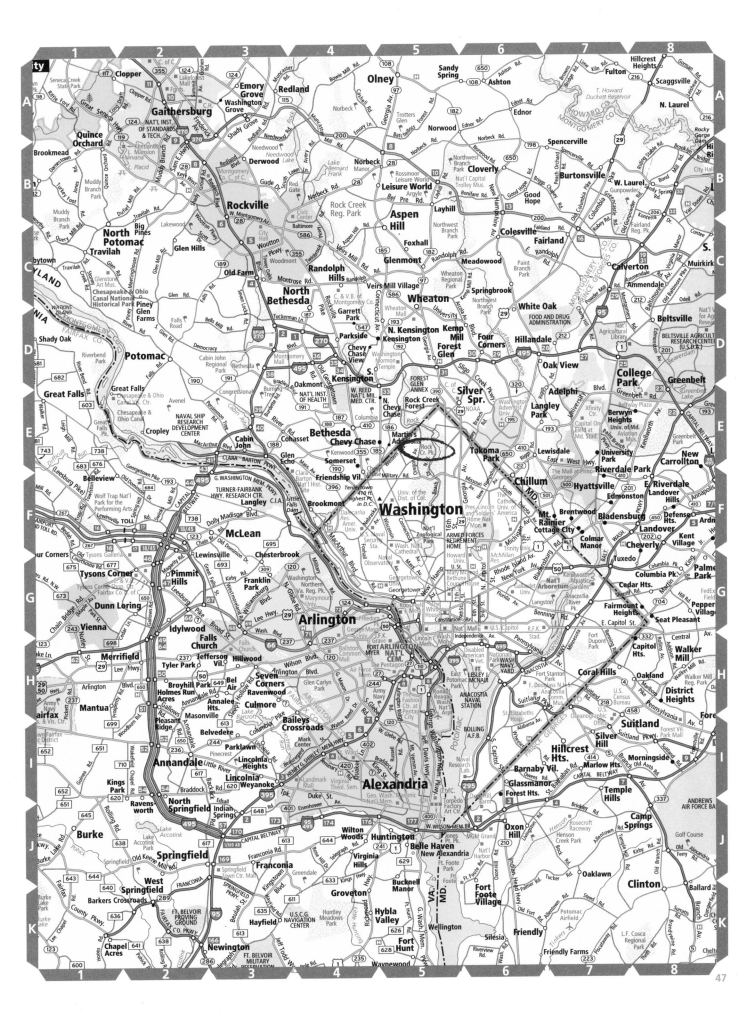

West Virginia
The Mountain State

Wish you could live without screens and devices? The wish is real in Green Bank, WV, the heart of the National Radio Quiet Zone. No wi-fi, cell reception, radio, TV... *ah silence*. Green Bank is home to the world's largest, steerable radio telescope that detects electromagnetic waves from far-away galaxies. Any slight electronic device emission can interfere. While you're incommunicado, go tour this awesome telescope at the Green Bank Observatory. Be sure to pack your road atlas because you can't use a GPS to get there.

How To Map It!™

Use the list below to seek a challenge found on the map and cross it off as you go. **Instructions on page 5.**

Her Town	His Town	Villes	State Parks	Counties
☒ Green Bank F,8	❑ Ashton __ __	❑ Churchville __ __	❑ Audra __ __	❑ Braxton __ __
❑ Ashley __ __	❑ Bud __ __	❑ Cottageville __ __	❑ Babcock __ __	❑ Calhoun __ __
❑ Belle __ __	❑ Calvin __ __	❑ Fosterville __ __	❑ Beartown __ __	❑ Clay __ __
❑ Beverly __ __	❑ Cameron __ __	❑ Harrisville __ __	❑ Cabwaylingo __ __	❑ Doddridge __ __
❑ Blair __ __	❑ Carl __ __	❑ Huttonsville __ __	❑ Cedar Cr. __ __	❑ Fayette __ __
❑ Chloe __ __	❑ Elton __ __	❑ Jarvisville __ __	❑ Chief Logan __ __	❑ Greenbrier __ __
❑ Coco __ __	❑ Gilbert __ __	❑ Kiahsville __ __	❑ Greenbrier S.F. __ __	❑ Jackson __ __
❑ Corinne __ __	❑ Jeffrey __ __	❑ Loudenville __ __	❑ Hawks Nest __ __	❑ Logan __ __
❑ Diana __ __	❑ Jesse __ __	❑ Monterville __ __	❑ Holly River __ __	❑ Mason __ __
❑ Eleanor __ __	❑ Julian __ __	❑ Nestorville __ __	❑ Kumbrabow __ __	❑ McDowell __ __
❑ Elizabeth __ __	❑ Leon __ __	❑ Pettyville __ __	❑ Moncove Lake __ __	❑ Mingo __ __
❑ Helen __ __	❑ Leopold __ __	❑ Pineville __ __	❑ North Bend __ __	❑ Pleasants __ __
❑ Jodie __ __	❑ Milton __ __	❑ Rivesville __ __	❑ Pipestem Resort __ __	❑ Putnam __ __
❑ Kenna __ __	❑ Rupert __ __	❑ Sissonville __ __	❑ Seneca S.F. __ __	❑ Roane __ __
❑ Leslie __ __	❑ Seth __ __	❑ Sistersville __ __	❑ Twin Falls Resort __ __	❑ Summers __ __
❑ Myrtle __ __	❑ Sherman __ __	❑ Tallmansville __ __	❑ Tygart Lakes __ __	❑ Tyler __ __
❑ Sabine __ __	❑ Tanner __ __	❑ Taylorville __ __	❑ Valley Falls __ __	❑ Upshur __ __
❑ Shirley __ __	❑ Troy __ __	❑ Verdunville __ __	❑ Watoga __ __	❑ Wetzel __ __
❑ Sophia __ __	❑ Wayne __ __	❑ Waiteville __ __		❑ Wyoming __ __

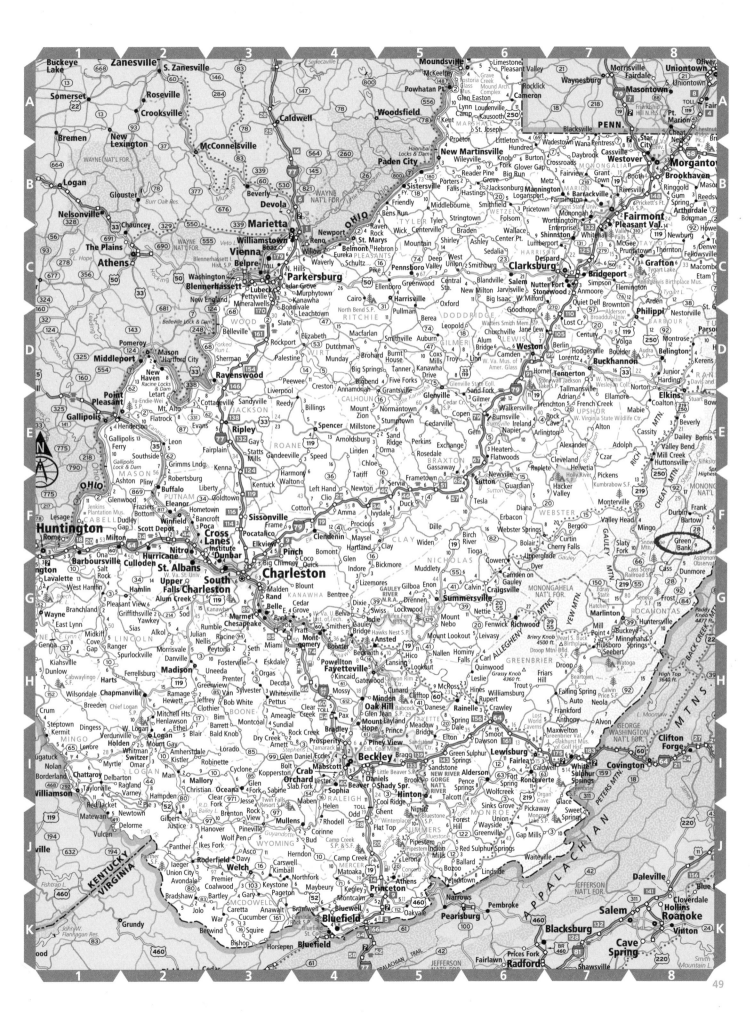

Wisconsin
The Badger State

Just what goes on behind Delaney's Surplus in Baraboo, WI? Just your everyday Forevertron. Forever-what? Dr. Evermor's scrap metal sculpture garden of creatures made from imagination and industrial salvage, musical instruments, some Thomas Edison bipolar dynamos (!), a NASA decontamination chamber, gas pump nozzles and who knows what else. The centerpiece is the 160-foot wide Forevertron that will someday transport Dr. Evermor to the heavens. It's a treat for eyes and ears, but hurry, who knows when he'll take off.

How To Map It!™
Use the list below to seek a challenge found on the map and cross it off as you go. **Instructions on page 5.**

Villes
- ☒ Baraboo **H,2**
- ☐ Auroraville ___ ___
- ☐ Belleville ___ ___
- ☐ Bloomville ___ ___
- ☐ Clintonville ___ ___
- ☐ Daleyville ___ ___
- ☐ Dexterville ___ ___
- ☐ Ellisville ___ ___
- ☐ Flintville ___ ___
- ☐ Greenville ___ ___
- ☐ Harrisville ___ ___
- ☐ Loganville ___ ___
- ☐ Mayville ___ ___
- ☐ Nelsonville ___ ___
- ☐ Postville ___ ___
- ☐ Rozellville ___ ___
- ☐ Saxeville ___ ___
- ☐ Stangelville ___ ___
- ☐ Stetsonville ___ ___

Rivers
- ☐ Baraboo ___ ___
- ☐ Big Rib ___ ___
- ☐ Crawfish ___ ___
- ☐ Eau Claire ___ ___
- ☐ *Fox ___ , ___ ___
- ☐ Manitowoc ___ ___
- ☐ Mecan ___ ___
- ☐ Milwaukee ___ ___
- ☐ Oconto ___ ___
- ☐ *Pine ___ , ___ ___
- ☐ Plover ___ ___
- ☐ Prairie ___ ___
- ☐ Rock ___ ___
- ☐ Sugar ___ ___
- ☐ Waupaca ___ ___
- ☐ Wisconsin ___ ___
- ☐ Wolf ___ ___
- ☐ Yahara ___ ___
- ☐ Yellow ___ ___

State Parks
- ☐ Aztalan ___ ___
- ☐ Big Foot Bch. ___ ___
- ☐ Buckhorn ___ ___
- ☐ Copper Culture ___ ___
- ☐ Council Grounds ___ ___
- ☐ Devil's Lake ___ ___
- ☐ Governor Dodge ___ ___
- ☐ Harrington Beach ___ ___
- ☐ Hartman Cr. ___ ___
- ☐ High Cliff ___ ___
- ☐ Kohler-Andrae ___ ___
- ☐ Mill Bluff ___ ___
- ☐ Mirror Lake ___ ___
- ☐ New Glarus Woods ___ ___
- ☐ R. Bong S.R.A. ___ ___
- ☐ Tower Hill ___ ___
- ☐ Yellowstone Lake ___ ___

Lakes
- ☐ Castle Rock L. ___ ___
- ☐ Chute Pnd. ___ ___
- ☐ Greer L. ___ ___
- ☐ High Falls Res. ___ ___
- ☐ L. Butte des Morts ___ ___
- ☐ L. Geneva ___ ___
- ☐ L. Kegonsa ___ ___
- ☐ L. Koshkonong ___ ___
- ☐ L. Mendota ___ ___
- ☐ L. Poygan ___ ___
- ☐ Lake Winnebago ___ ___
- ☐ Lake Wisconsin ___ ___
- ☐ Petenwell L. ___ ___
- ☐ Rock L. ___ ___
- ☐ Rush L. ___ ___
- ☐ Shawano L. ___ ___

Counties
- ☐ Adams ___ ___
- ☐ Calumet ___ ___
- ☐ Dodge ___ ___
- ☐ Door ___ ___
- ☐ Fond du Lac ___ ___
- ☐ Green ___ ___
- ☐ Jefferson ___ ___
- ☐ Juneau ___ ___
- ☐ Lafayette ___ ___
- ☐ Langlade ___ ___
- ☐ Marquette ___ ___
- ☐ Outagamie ___ ___
- ☐ Portage ___ ___
- ☐ Rock ___ ___
- ☐ Sauk ___ ___
- ☐ Shawano ___ ___
- ☐ Taylor ___ ___
- ☐ Walworth ___ ___
- ☐ Washington ___ ___

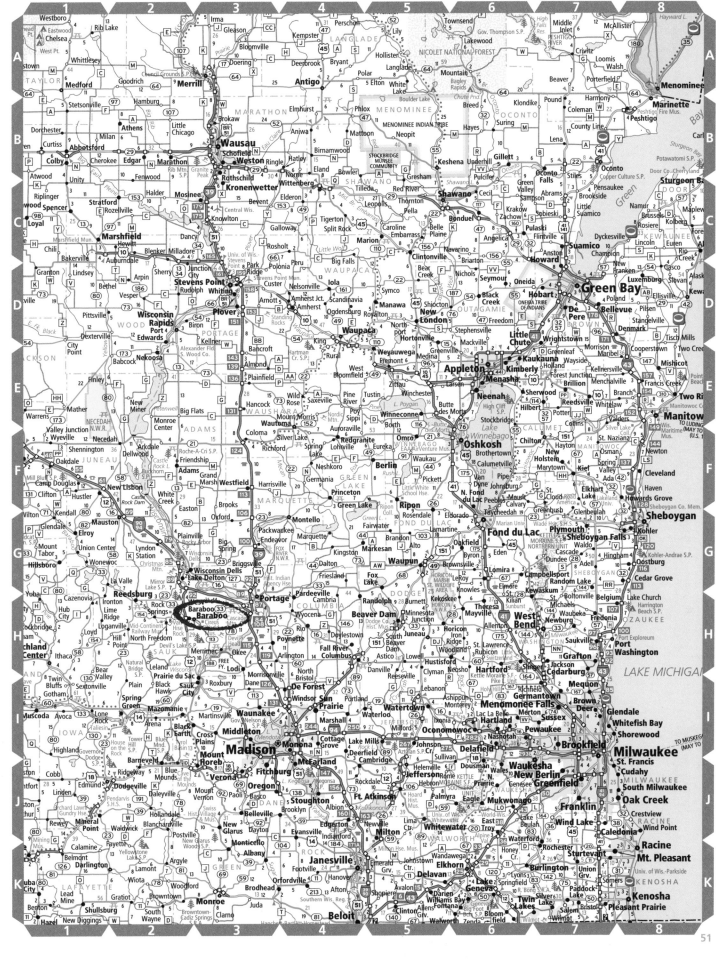

Wyoming
The Equality State

Relax. Go with the flow. Sounds easy, unless you're in the Bridger-Teton National Forest in Moran, WY. Here is where North Two Ocean Creek, on the continental divide, breaks into two streams, one flowing left to the Atlantic (via the Yellowstone, Missouri and Mississippi Rivers) and one flowing right to the Pacific (via the Snake and Columbia Rivers.) Which way will you go?

How To Map It! ™
Use the list below to seek a challenge found on the map and cross it off as you go. **Instructions on page 5.**

Towns
- ☒ Moran D,1
- ❏ Albany ___ ___
- ❏ Bar Nunn ___ ___
- ❏ Big Horn ___ ___
- ❏ Buffalo ___ ___
- ❏ Cokeville ___ ___
- ❏ Crowheart ___ ___
- ❏ Elk Mountain ___ ___
- ❏ Foxpark ___ ___
- ❏ Frontier ___ ___
- ❏ Greybull ___ ___
- ❏ Hanna ___ ___
- ❏ Hudson ___ ___
- ❏ Mammoth ___ ___
- ❏ Meeteetse ___ ___
- ❏ Moose ___ ___
- ❏ Owl Creek ___ ___
- ❏ Reliance ___ ___
- ❏ Spotted Horse ___ ___
- ❏ Ten Sleep ___ ___
- ❏ Ucross ___ ___

Creeks & Rivers
- ❏ *Bighorn ___ , ___ ___
- ❏ Big Sandy ___ ___
- ❏ Bitter Cr. ___ ___
- ❏ Blacks Fk. ___ ___
- ❏ Crazy Woman Cr. ___ ___
- ❏ *Green ___ ___ , ___ ___
- ❏ Greybull ___ ___
- ❏ Greys ___ ___
- ❏ Hams Fk. ___ ___
- ❏ Little Muddy ___ ___
- ❏ Medicine Bow ___ ___
- ❏ Muddy Cr. ___ ___
- ❏ Nowood ___ ___
- ❏ Powder ___ ___
- ❏ S. Fk. Shoshone ___ ___
- ❏ Salt Cr. ___ ___
- ❏ Snake ___ ___
- ❏ Sweetwater ___ ___
- ❏ Wind ___ ___

Lakes
- ❏ Alcova Res. ___ ___
- ❏ Boulder L. ___ ___
- ❏ Boysen Res. ___ ___
- ❏ Buffalo Bill Res. ___ ___
- ❏ Bull L. ___ ___
- ❏ Cooper L. ___ ___
- ❏ Eden Res. ___ ___
- ❏ Flaming Gorge Res. ___ ___
- ❏ Fontenelle Res. ___ ___
- ❏ Fremont L. ___ ___
- ❏ Jackson L. ___ ___
- ❏ L. Hattie ___ ___
- ❏ Lewis L. ___ ___
- ❏ New Fk. L. ___ ___
- ❏ Ocean L. ___ ___
- ❏ Pathfinder Res. ___ ___
- ❏ Seminoe Res. ___ ___
- ❏ Shoshone L. ___ ___
- ❏ Willow L. ___ ___
- ❏ Yellowstone Lake ___ ___

Mountains
- ❏ Blackhall Mtn ___ ___
- ❏ Cedar Mtn. ___ ___
- ❏ Cloud Pk. ___ ___
- ❏ Continental Pk. ___ ___
- ❏ Crescent Mtn. ___ ___
- ❏ Eagle Pk. ___ ___
- ❏ Elk Mtn. ___ ___
- ❏ Essex Mtn. ___ ___
- ❏ Fortress Mtn. ___ ___
- ❏ Heart Mtn. ___ ___
- ❏ Hoback Pk. ___ ___
- ❏ Ice Cave Mtn. ___ ___
- ❏ Mt. Holmes ___ ___
- ❏ North Butte ___ ___
- ❏ Pelican Cone ___ ___
- ❏ Pinnacle Pk. ___ ___
- ❏ Sheets Mtn. ___ ___
- ❏ The Thunderer ___ ___
- ❏ Whiskey Mtn. ___ ___
- ❏ Younts Pk. ___ ___

Counties
- ❏ Albany ___ ___
- ❏ Big Horn ___ ___
- ❏ Carbon ___ ___
- ❏ Fremont ___ ___
- ❏ Hot Springs ___ ___
- ❏ Johnson ___ ___
- ❏ Lincoln ___ ___
- ❏ Natrona ___ ___
- ❏ Park ___ ___
- ❏ Sheridan ___ ___
- ❏ Sublette ___ ___
- ❏ Sweetwater ___ ___
- ❏ Teton ___ ___
- ❏ Uinta ___ ___
- ❏ Washakie ___ ___

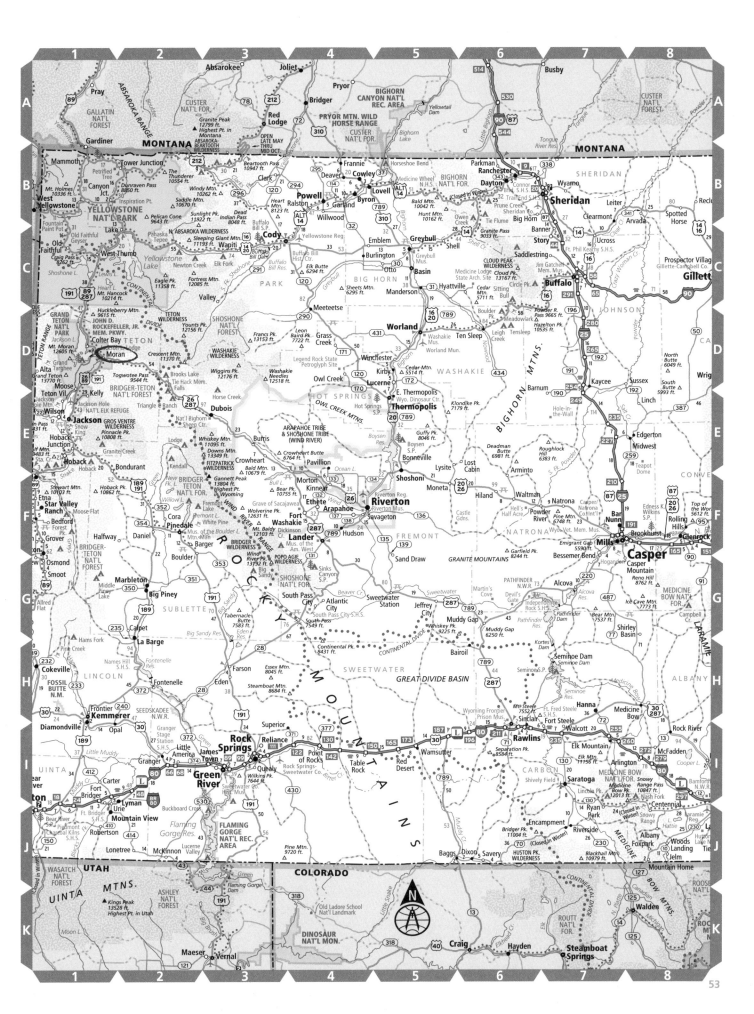

Solutions

Nevada

Towns

I5 Goldfield
J8 Ash Springs
D6 Beowawe
E8 Cherry Creek
G7 Duckwater
D1 Empire
F7 Eureka
G4 Gabbs
J5 Gold Point
J8 Hiko
A7 Jarbridge
G4 Lone
D3 Lovelock
H5 Manhattan
E2 Nixon
A7 Owyhee
A4 Paradise Valley
F1 Stagecoach
H6 Warm Springs

Creeks & Rivers

G7 Bull Creek
A6 Bull Run
D7 Dixie
D8 Franklin
H6 Hot Creek
C5, C7 *Humbolt
A3 Kings
B2 Leonard
C6 Maggie Cr.
A8 Marys
B2 Mud Meadow
E6 Pine Cr.
A4, B3 *Quinn
E5 Reese
C6 Rock Creek
E4 Spring Cr.
C7 Susie Cr.
F2 Walker
H8, J8 *White

Lakes

B8 Bishop Creek Reservoir
F3 Carson Lake
B5 Chimney Dam Res.
K8 Desert Lake
D8 Franklin Lake
J7 Groom Lake
F2 Lahontan Res.
A1 Massacre Lake
I5 Mud Lake
A1 New Year Lake
E7 Newark Lake
D1 Pyramid Lake
E8 Ruby Lake

C3 Rye Patch Reservoir
A7 Wild Horse Res.
D2 Winnemucca Lake
K7 Yucca Lake

Mountains & Peeks

J7 Bald Mountain
H5 Bald Mtn.
B4 Bloody Run Pk.
D3 Buffalo Mtn.
I5 Cactus Pk.
F7 Diamond Pk.
A3 Disaster Peak
C6 Emigrant Pass
I4 Emigrant Pk.
A4 Granite Pk.
K5 Grapevine Pk.
B5 Hot Springs Pk.
G6 Ninemile Peak
D1 Pah-Rum Pk.
F7 Pancake Summit
H4 Pilot Peak
K6 Shoshone Peak
H7 Troy Pk.

Counties

F3 Churchhill
G1 Douglas
B7 Elko
I4 Esmeralda
E6 Eureka
B3 Humboldt
E5 Lander
G2 Lyon
H3 Mineral
I6 Nye
D3 Pershing
F1 Storey
C1 Washoe
F8 White Pine

New Hampshire

Towns

I7 Portsmouth
D6 Albany
E4 Beebe River
B6 Cascade
F3 Dorchester
C5 Fabyan
A5 Groveton
I4 Henniker
H5 Kelleys Corner
J4 Lyndeborough
A6 Milan
I6 Newmarket
F6 Ossipee
I5 Pembroke

H3 Potter Place
E5 Sandwich
G4 Tilton
H2 Unity
D4 Woodstock

Creeks & Rivers

C3 Ammonoosuc
K2 Ashuelot
E4 Baker
A6 Chickwolnepy
I2 Cold
E2 Connecticut
J3 Contoocook
C6 Ellis
J7 Exeter
B5 Isreal
E5 Mad
H4 Merrimack
F4 Pemigewasset
F6 Pine
D6 Saco
G4 Smith
K4 Souhegan
H2 Sugar
D6 Swift

Lakes

I7 Bellamy Res.
H6 Bow Lake
G5 Crystal Lake
I4 Drew Lake
F2 Goose Pd.
I2 Highland Lake
K6 Island Pond
D3 Lake Tarleton
G6 Lake Wentworth
F2 Mascoma L.
F4 Newfound Lake
J2 Nubanusit Lake
F6 Ossipee Lake
J2 Silver Lake
F5 Squam Lake
A6 Success Pond
H3 Sunapee Lake
I6 Union L.
I4 Weare Reservoir

Hills, Mills & Villes

I5 Bow Mills
K2 Bowkerville
G1 Cornish Mills
J6 Danville
H4 Davisville
I1 Drewsville
I5 Gossville
K4 Greenville
J3 Harrisville

G4 Hill
H2 Kellyville
J2 Munsonville
E3 Orfordville
C3 Parker Hill
G7 Sanbornville
E7 Snowville
C4 Sugar Hill
E5 Waterville Valley
K6 Westville

State Parks

I5 Bear Brook
I4 Clough
C5 Crawford Notch
D6 Echo Lake
G5 Ellacoya
B4 Forest Lake
D4 Franconia Notch
J3 Greenfield
J6 Kingston
K3 Monadnock
B5 Moose Brook
H2 Mt. Sunapee
I2 Pilsbury
K1 Pisgah
H3 Rollins
J8 Rye Harbor
K4 Silver Lake
H3 Wadleigh
F3 Wellington

New Jersey

Towns

D7 Hoboken
K3 Chambers Corners
H6 Colts Neck
B3 Cranberry Lake
J4 Cream Ridge
H3 Dutch Neck
B5 Green Pond
K7 Holiday City
K3 Jobstown
J7 Lake Como
E4 Liberty Corner
C5 Lincoln Park
H2 Mount Airy
C4 Mount Hope
F1 Mount Pleasant
D5 Short Hills
C2 Vienna
H6 Wickatunk
I4 Windsor
B2 Yellow Frame

55

Solutions

D2	La Fargeville
F3	Lowville
F2	Mannsville
I8	Northville
B6	Parishville
I1	Pennellville
C4	Richville
F3	Tylersville
B5	Unionville
J4	Waterville
H4	Westernville

State Parks

H1	Battle Island
D1	Burnham Point
J3	Chittenango Falls
A5	Coles Cr.
H4	Delta Lake
C2	Dewolf Pt.
B4	Eel Weir
K1	Fillmore Glen
K6	Glimmerglass
I2	Green Lakes
C5	Higley Flow
C3	Kring Point
H4	Pixley Falls
G1	Sandy Island Beach
G1	Selkirk Shores
F1	Southwick Beach
B4	St. Lawrence
I3	Verona Beach
E1	Westcott Beach

Lakes

D8	Ampersand Lake
F6	Big Moose Lake
E6	Bog Lake
E8	Catlin L.
E6	Cranberry Lake
H5	Hinckley Res.
D4	L. Bonaparte
H8	L. Pleasant
B8	L. Titus
E7	Lake Eaton
E7	Long Lake
B8	Loon Lake
H3	Mad
C4	Mud L.
B5	Norwood Lake
I2	Oneida Lake
D2	Perch L.
E8	Rich L.
G5	Woodhull Lake
D3	Yellow L.

North Carolina

Burgs & Hills

K6	Sunset Beach
I5	Abbottsburg
G4	Arran Hills
A5	Bethel Hill
C4	Chapel Hill
D1	Jackson Hill
B6	Louisburg
D4	New Hill
A2	Oregon Hill
G6	Parkersburg
F8	Pink Hill
B4	Prospect Hill
G7	Rose Hill
G6	Salemburg
E8	Snow Hill
D8	Stantonsburg
B3	Williamsburg

Creeks & Rivers

I7	Black
E5, I6	*Cape Fear
I6	Colly Cr.
A1	Dan
D3	Deep
B7	Fishing Cr.
B5	Flat
C4	Haw
G3	Lumber
I8	N.E. Cape Fear
E7	Neuse
G7	Six Runs Cr.
F6, H6	*South
C7	Tar

Villes

A5	Allensville
F1	Ansonville
G5	Autryville
I4	Barnesville
B8	Brinkleyville
A3	Casville
B7	Centerville
D2	Franklinville
F4	Johnsonville
C3	Kimesville
C6	Mapleville
D5	Morrisville
E8	Pikeville
A1	Prestonville
I4	Proctorville
A6	Townsville
A3	Yanceyville

Lakes

E1	Badin L.
H6	Bay Tree Lake
B1	Belews L.
G1	Blewett Falls Lake
C5	Falls Lake
D1	High Rock L.
G6	Horseshoe Lake
A4	Hyco Lake
E1	L. Tillery
B2	L. Townsend
A7	Lake Gaston
B5	Lake Michie
J6	Lake Waccamaw
H5	Little Singletary L.
H6	White Lake

Counties

I6	Bladen
J6	Brunswick
A3	Caswell
J5	Columbus
B5	Durham
C2	Guilford
E4	Harnett
F4	Hoke
E3	Moore
C7	Nash
B4	Orange
D2	Randolph
G2	Richmond
F6	Sampson
G3	Scotland
A6	Vance
E7	Wayne

North Dakota

His Town

I1	Bismarck
I5	Adrian
H7	Arthur
J8	Barney
D2	Barton
C4	Calvin
G7	Clifford
D4	Clyde
J6	Elliott
F2	Guthrie
I7	Horace
H7	Hunter
G5	Jessie
I7	Leonard
C6	Leroy
D6	Milton
D3	Mylo
D1	Russell
I7	Sheldon

Her Town

I6	Alice
F6	Aneta
K4	Ashley
D6	Crystal
H6	Dazey
F4	Flora
D1	Gardena
C4	Hannah
G6	Hope
G5	Juanita
I6	Kathryn
I5	Marion
I2	McKenzie
I3	Medina
D6	Olga
H7	Page
G6	Sharon
E3	Silva
J6	Verona

Lakes

G4	Arrowwood Lake
J3	Beaver Lake
G1	Blue Lake
E3	Cranberry Lake
G1	Crooked Lake
E4	Dry Lake
J3	Green Lake
H3	Horsehead Lake
I3	Lake George
K7	Lake Tewaukon
D3, I2	*Long Lake
E1	North Lake
C4	Rock Lake
D2	Round Lake
C4	Rush Lake
E2	Smoky Lake
F1	Strawberry Lake
F5	Stump Lake
G1	Turtle Lake

Creeks & Rivers

K2	Beaver Cr.
H7	Elm
E6	Forest
F6	Goose
H4, J6	*James
H6	Maple
H1, K2	*Missouri
D2	Ox Cr.
G4	Pipestem Cr.
D7, G8, J8	*Red
H7	Rush
D6	S. Br. Park
G6, J7	*Sheyenne
E1	Souris
D6	Tongue

Solutions

D8 Christie
G5 Hanna
H2 Joy
H1 Katie
H4 Lula
C6 Mazie
H8 Octavia
J6 Oleta
B5 Ramona
C7 Rose
H5 Savanna
B5 Vera
F5 Vivian
H8 Zoe

State Parks

G5 Arrowhead
I4 Boggy Depot
E7 Brushy Lake
B7 Disney Little Blue
E4 Dripping Springs
E7 Greenleaf
J8 Hochatown
J6 Hugo Lake
C4 Keystone
F1 Lake Thunderbird
G7 Lake Wister
E4 Okmulgee
A4 Osage Hills
G6 Robbers Cave
D6 Sequoyah Bay
C6 Snowdale
H7 Talimena
E7 Tenkiller
C4 Walnut Cr.

Counties

D8 Adair
J4 Bryan
J5 Choctaw
A6 Craig
D3 Creek
B7 Delaware
H1 Garvin
F7 Haskell
I3 Johnston
A1 Kay
G6 Latimer
H7 Le Flore
J1 Love
B1 Noble
D5 Okmulgee
H5 Pittsburg
I6 Pushmataha
C5 Rogers
G3 Seminole

His Town

G4 Allen
F7 Brent
G4 Calvin
F2 Dale
F4 Dustin
G3 Francis
I2 Gene Autry
D5 Geonard
K6 Grant
E5 Grayson
J6 Hugo
K1 Leon
D5 Leonard
E4 Mason
C1 Perry
E5 Preston
G4 Stuart
K8 Tom
I3 Troy

Lakes

B4 Birch Lake
A5 Copan Lake
F6 Eufaula Lake
D6 Ft. Gibson Lake
D4 Heyburn Lake
J6 Hugo Lake
A2 Kaw Lake
E1 Lake Arcadia
G5 Lake McAlester
J2 Lake Murray
G1 Lake Thunderbird
I5 McGee Creek Lake
B6 Oologah Lake
J7 Pine Creek Lake
H6 Sardis Lake
B4 Skiatook Lake
B2 Sooner Lake
E7 Tenkiller Ferry Lake
G8 Wister lake

Oregon

Her Town

D2 Yachats
B5 Aumsville
H7 Beaver Marsh
C5 Crabtree
E4 Crow
J5 Eagle Point
B3 Elk City
F3 Elkton
K7 Falcon Hts.
D6 Finn Rock
A2 Kernville
B2 Otter Rock
C2 Seal Rock
C5 Sodaville

A6 Three Lynx
J3 Wilderville
I3 Wolf Creek
C4 Wren

Rivers

I7 Annie
J4 Applegate
F4 Big
D5 Calapooia
A7 Clackamas
C8 Deschutes
J3 Illinois
K6 Jenny
G5 Little
K8 Lost
F8 Paulina
A6 Pudding
I3, J5 *Rogue
F5 Sharps
J2 Silver
F3 Umpqua
B8 Warm Springs
A8 White

Campsites

K4 Beaver Sulphur
G5 Bogus Creek
F5 Cedar Creek
D7 Devils Lake
E7 Dutch Oven
G5 Eagle Rock
A8 Frog Lake
D6 Horse Creek
F1 Horsefall
E2 Lagoon
C6 Lost Prairie
D7 Paradise
J1 Quosatana
J6 Rainbow Bay
I2 Squaw Lake
I5 Threehorn
C6 Trout Creek
J6 Whiskey Springs

Lakes

J6 Aspen Lake
D6 Blue River Lake
H6 Crater Lake
E5 Dorena Lake
D3 Fern Ridge Lake
J6 Fish Lake
C5 Foster Lake
K5 Hyatt Res.
C8 Lake Billy Chinook
E7 Lava Lake
G6 Lemolo Lake
I5 Lost Creek Lake
E2 Siltcoos Lake

C7 Suttle Lake
F2 Tenmile Lake
F6 Waldo Lake

State Parks

D3 Alderwood St. Wayside
B2 Beverly Beach
C5 Cascadia
C6 Detroit Lake S.R.A.
E5 Elijah Bristow
K1 Harris Beach
F8 LaPine
J1 Otter Point St. Rec. Site
A2 Robert Straub
B5 Silver Falls
G1 Sunset Bay
C8 The Cove Palisades
D8 Tumalo
J4 Val. of the Rogue
C2 Yachats St. Rec Area

Pennsylvania

Hills & Mills

I3 Dauphin
B3 Balls Mills
I5 Bunker Hill
J3 Camp Hill
G1 Cuba Mills
H2 Donnally Mills
F3 Globe Mills
B1 Jersey Mills
A3 Marsh Hill
G2 Oakland Mills
A1 Oregon Hill
D7 Pond Hill
A8 Russell Hill
I6 Sand Hill
H1 Spruce Hill
I7 State Hill
D6 Summer Hill
J8 Terre Hill

Villes

F7 Brandonville
D2 Collomsville
E5 Danville
A8 Eatonville
J7 Farmersville
A5 Forksville
I5 Grantville
C8 Huntsville
K2 Idaville
C7 Koonsville
C8 Larksville
E6 Mainville
D5 Millville
B2 Perryville
B2 Quiggleville

I4 Rockville
I4 Shellsville
E1 Tylersville
B1 Waterville
K3 Wellsville

Creeks & Rivers

E2, I1 *Buffalo Cr.
B7 Bowman Cr.
E7 Catawissa Cr.
H4 Clark Cr.
C6 Fishing Cr.
D6 Huntington Cr.
G1 Jacks Cr.
B2 Larrys Cr.
C1 Lick Run
I2 Little Juniatá Cr.
B4 Loyalsock Cr.
A3 Lycoming Cr.
F4 Mahanoy Cr.
F2 Penns Cr.
E6 Roaring Cr.
G7 Schuylkill
J5 Swatara Cr.
D3 White Deer Cr.
G4 Wiconisco Cr.

State Parks

D1 Bald Eagle S.F.
I1 Colonial Denning
K4 Gifford Pinchot
H2 Little Buffalo
B1 Little Pine
F7 Locust Lake
D3 Milton
C7 Moon Lake S.F.
D8 Nescopeck
K2 Pine Grv. Furnace
F1 Poe Paddy
D2 Ravensburg
F1 Reeds Gap
K5 Samuel S. Lewis
E3 Shikellamy
C3 Susquehanna
F7 Tuscarora
A5 Worlds End

Counties

H8 Berks
D6 Columbia
J2 Cumberland
I4 Dauphin
G2 Juniata
K7 Lancaster
H5 Lebanon
C8 Luzerne
B2 Lycoming
F1 Mifflin
D4 Montour
F4 Northumberland

I2 Perry
H6 Schuylkill
F3 Snyder
B6 Sullivan
E2 Union
A7 Wyoming
K4 York

South Carolina

Hills & Mills

D6 Bishopville
H7 Beverly Hills
F1 Clarks Hill
D2 Cross Hill
A5 Fort Mill
G6 Holly Hill
G8 Honey Hill
A1 Inman Mills
C5 Liberty Hill
B3 Monarch Mill
B4 Rock Hill
C7 Society Hill
C5 Spring Mills
D3 Stoney Hill
C1 Watts Mills
C4 Winnsboro Mills

Creeks & Rivers

I6 Ashepoo
F7 Black
D2 Bush
J5 Combahee
F5 Congaree
I6 Edisto
G5 Four Hole
D8 Great Pee Dee
E1 Long Cane Cr.
D6 Lynches
F3 N. Fk. Edisto
B3 Pacolet
G8 Santee
H3 Savannah
E1 Stevens Cr.
B2 Tyger
E5 Wateree

Lakes

C5 Fishing Cr. Res.
D2 L. Greenwood
G6 L. Marion
G7 L. Moultrie
E3 L. Murray
C7 L. Robinson
A4 L. Wylie
C4 Monticello Res.
G3 Par Pond
C5 Wateree L.

Counties

I3 Allendale
F2 Edgefield
E8 Florence
J4 Jasper
E3 Lexington
C8 Marlboro
D2 Newberry
F8 Williamsburg

Villes

C4 Beckhamville
G4 Blackville
I7 Centerville
C7 Dovesville
A2 Fingerville
I4 Gillisonville
G6 Harleyville
C7 Hartsville
D4 Jenkinsville
E7 Mayesville
C2 Mountville
E1 Parksville
F6 Paxville
J4 Robertville
G5 Rowesville
G7 Russellville
A1 Tigerville
I4 Varnville
B1 Woodville

State Parks

F3 Aiken S.N.A.
G3 Barnwell
B7 Cheraw
B3 Chester
H5 Colleton
B2 Croft S.N.A.
D3 Dreher I. S.R.A.
J6 Edisto Beach
H6 Givhans Ferry
J6 Hunting Island
D2 L. Greenwood S.R.A.
I4 Lake Warren
E5 Manchester S.F.
D6 N.R. Goodale
A1 Paris Mtn.
F6 Poinsett
C7 Sand Hills S.F.
F6 Santee

South Dakota

His Town

E7 De Smet
D5 Ashton
D6 Bradley
E8 Bruce
H2 Carter
G8 Chester

G8 Ellis
H6 Ethan
B5 Frederick
H5 Harrison
F7 Howard
I5 Marty
C8 Marvin
H7 Parker
E2 Pierre
G7 Spencer
D8 Troy
B8 Victor
F5 Virgil
D7 Wallace

Creeks & Rivers

E8 Big Sioux
H6 Choteau Cr.
E8 Deer
H3 Dog Ear Cr.
B5 Elm
E5, H7 *James
H2 Keya Paha
H1 Little White
G4 Missouri
C6 Mud Cr.
B2 Oak Cr.
E2 Okobojo Cr.
H5 Platte Cr.
F5 Sand Cr.
G5 Smith Cr.
E4 Turtle Cr.
I8 Vermillion
F2 White Clay
E4 Wolf Cr.

Lakes

C7 Bitter L.
E5 Cottonwood L.
B5 Elm L.
E6 L. Bryon
H4 L. Francis Case
F8 L. Madison
F7 L. Whitewood
D2 Lake Oahe
B5 Mud L. Res.
G4 Platte L.
G4 Red L.
C5 Richmond L.
B3 Salt L.
C3 Spring L.
D3 Stone L.
C3 Swan L.
C7 Waubay L.
G5 White L.

Her Town

E8 Astoria
F8 Aurora
I6 Avon

Solutions

C5 Chelsea
C7 Eden
G7 Emery
D7 Florence
D7 Hazel
H6 Kaylor
B4 Leola
C7 Lily
C5 Mina
E3 Onida
H5 Ravinia
F7 Romona
H1 Rosebud
C7 Roslyn

State Parks

F3 Buryanek S.R.A.
D5 Fisher Grv.
C2 Indian Cr. S.R.A.
F3 Lake Louise S.R.A.
E8 Lake Poinsett S.R.A.
G7 Lake Vermillion S.R.A.
C1 Little Moreau S.R.A.
C4 Mina Lake S.R.A.
H8 Newton Hills
E7 Oakwood Lakes
E2 Okobojo Pt. S.R.A.
H5 Pease Cr. S.R.A.
D7 Pelican Lake S.R.A.
B6 Roy Lake
B7 Sica Hollow
I6 Springfield S.R.A.
I8 Union Grove
F3 W. Bend S.R.A.

Tennessee

Towns

D5 Nashville
H8 Alto
F1 Bible Hill
H1 Burnt Church
I5 Cash Point
G5 Chapel Hill
E2 Cuba Landing
D8 Difficult
G2 Flatwoods
F4 Fly
C6 Fountain Head
I3 Iron City
G3 Mount Joy
C6 New Deal
G8 New Union
F2 Only
C4 Pleasant View
D7 Rome
C3, F7 *Shiloh
F1 Sugar Tree
C6 White House

Rivers

E1 Big Sandy
F2 Buffalo
C4 Cumberland
E2, G5 *Duck
F7 E. Fk. Stones
I6 Elk
D4 Harpeth
E3 Piney
I3 Shoal
E2, G1 *Tennessee

Lakes

E6 J. Percy Priest L.
C2 L. Barkley
G7 Normandy Lake
D6 Old Hickory L.
H6 Tims Ford L.
H8 Woods Res.

State Parks

D6 Bledsoe Cr.
E7 Cedars of Lebanon
H3 David Crockett
C4 Dunbar Cave
E8 Edgar Evins
D4 Harpeth River
G5 Henry Horton
E2 Johnsonville
G3 Lewis
D6 Long Hunter
D3 Montgomery Bell
D1 Nathan Bedford Forrest
C1 Paris Landing
I1 Pickwick Landing
C4 Port Royal
C2 Stewart
H7 Tims Ford

Villes

F6 Almaville
H6 Belleville
H4 Campbellsville
F3 Centerville
G1 Decaturville
F6 Eagleville
I5 Fayetteville
E6 Gladeville
C7 Hartsville
H3 Henryville
E1 Johnsonville
D6 Leeville
F2 Lobelville
D1 Manlyville
C6 Mitchellville
E5 Nolensville
G1 Perryville
F7 Readyville
D1 Springville

G8 Summitville
G6 Unionville

Counties

E1 Benton
G7 Coffee
G1 Decatur
D3 Dickson
I7 Franklin
H4 Giles
I1 Hardin
F3 Hickman
D2 Houston
I6 Lincoln
H5 Marshall
H7 Moore
F2 Perry
C5 Robertson
F6 Rutherford
C2 Stewart
C6 Sumner
C7 Trousdale
H2 Wayne
D7 Wilson

Texas

Hills & Springs

I6 Houston
I5 Chappell Hill
A7 Dalby Springs
I1 Dripping Springs
B6 Forest Hill
I4 Gay Hill
J3 High Hill
C7 Laird Hill
H1 Liberty Hill
I8 Moss Hill
C5 Myrtle Springs
A1 Park Springs
C5 Payne Springs
E4 Prairie Hill
J4 Rek Hill
I5 Rolling Hills
K1 Sutherland Springs
I1 The Hills
C1 Thorp Spring

Rivers

J1 Blanco
G4, K7 *Brazos
F1 Leon
G3 Little
E2 N. Bosque
H5 Navasota
F8 Neches
D5, H8 *Trinity

Lakes

C4 Cedar Cr. Res.
E5 Fairfield L.
A1 L. Bridgeport
H6 L. Conroe
F4 L. Limestone
G6 L. Livingston
D6 L. Palestine
B5 L. Tawakoni
B8 Lake O' The Pines

State Parks

I3 Bastrop
K6 Brazos Bend
I3 Buescher
D2 Cleburne
B8 Daingerfield
D1 Dinosaur Valley
E5 Fairfield Lake
E4 Ft. Parker
K8 Galveston Island
H6 Huntsville
B5 Lake Tawakoni
D2 Lake Whitney
J2 Lockhart
C8 Martin Cr. Lake
E1 Meridian
E7 Mission Tejas
F2 Mother Neff
K2 Palmetto
C5 Purtis Cr.
C7 Tyler

Villes

J4 Ammannsville
F2 Bruceville-Eddy
F5 Centerville
A7 Cookville
H4 Deanville
A4 Farmersville
F2 Gatesville
C8 Hallsville
G6 Huntsville
D6 Jacksonville
D8 Laneville
G5 Madisonville
K6 Needville
G2 Nolanville
B1 Poolville
C5 Prairieville
J4 Rutersville
I3 Smithville
H4 Somerville
E2 Turnersville

Counties

D6 Anderson
G1 Burnet
J4 Colorado

A2 Denton
D1 Erath
F3 Falls
K1 Guadalupe
D3 Hill
D1 Hood
A1 Jack
F5 Leon
I6 Montgomery
E4 Navarro
C1 Parker
G4 Robertson
H7 San Jacinto
G7 Trinity
B5 Van Zandt
G6 Walker
J6 Waller

Utah

Cities/Towns

B3 Midway
J2 Antimony
D3 Birdseye
C6 Bluebell
K5 Bullfrog
A3 Devils Slide
B7 Dry Fork
A8 Dutch John
A3 Echo
F5 Elmo
E3 Fountain Green
C5 Fruitland
E5 Helper
B4 Hideout
C4 Independence
E5 Kenilworth
G1 Meadow
C1 Rush Valley
E6 Sunnyside
E3 Wales

Creeks & Rivers

B7 Big Brush
E8 Bitter Cr.
F4 Cottonwood Cr.
I6 Dirty Devil
B5 Duchesne
K2 E. Fk. Sevier
K4 Escalante
D7, H7 *Green
I8 Hatch Wash
B6 Lake Fk.
H5 Muddy Cr.
E7 Nine Mile Cr.
I2 Otter Cr.
E5 Price
B4 Provo
B5 Rock Cr.
H6 San Rafael

J2 Sevier
B7 Whiterocks
E8 Willow Cr.

Mountains & Peaks

H4 Cedar Mtn.
I1 Delano Peak
A6 Gilbert Peak
H3 Hilgard Mtn.
D5 Indian Head Peak
B5 Mt. Agassiz
I1 Mt. Belknap
G2 Mt. Catherine
J2 Mt. Dutton
I5 Mt. Ellen
A8 Mt. Lena
J8 Mt. Linnaeus
D3 Mt. Nebo
I8 N. Sixshooter Peak
J8 Shay Mtn.
H5 Temple Mtn.
D2 Tintic Mtn.
G5 Window Blind Peak

State Parks

A1 Antelope Island
H7 Dead Horse Pt.
C3 Deer Cr.
A3 E. Canyon
H5 Goblin Valley
G6 Green River
F4 Huntington
B4 Jordanelle
K2 Kodachrome Basin
G4 Millsite
F3 Palisade
I2 Piute
B4 Rockport
D4 Scofield
B7 Steinaker
C3 Utah Lake
B3 Wasatch Mtn.
F2 Yuba

Lakes

C7 Bottle Hollow Res.
G1 Clear L.
F1 DMAD Res.
H3 Fish L.
F3 Gunnison Res.
F4 Joes Valley Res.
D2 Mona Res.
B5 Moon L.
B7 Oaks Park Res.
I2 Otter Cr. Res.
C7 Pelican L.
I2 Piute Res.
A4 Rockport L.
E4 Scofield Res.

C5 Starvation Res.
B8 Steinaker Res.
D4 Strawberry Res.
C3 Utah Lake

Vermont

Villes

D4 Stowe
G5 Beanville
I1 Blissville
F5 Cookville
J3 Cuttingsville
I6 Danville
J4 Felchville
H4 Gaysville
G3 Granville
J3 Healdville
A4 Hectorville
E3 Irasville
C3 Jeffersonville
D2 Jonesville
C7 Lyndonville
J4 Proctorsville
E4 Putnanville
I5 Taftsville
J3 Tarbellville
B3 Waterville
F5 Websterville

Creeks & Rivers

B3, C5, J4 *Black
A8 Black Br.
B7 Clyde
D6 Joes
D2 La Platte
C4 Lamoille
H1 Lemon Fair
E3 Mad
K2 Mettawee
J3 Mill
C7 Moose
B7 Nulhegan
C8 Paul
F3 Third Br.
G6 Waits
J2 Wells
G3, G4 *White
E4 Winooski

Mountains & Peaks

H3 Bloodroot Mtn.
G3 Bread Loaf Mtn.
C7 Burke Mtn.
H5 Gile Mtn.
A7 Gore Mtn.
C6 Granby Mtn.
C8 Harris Mtn.
A4 Jay Peak
I3 Killington Pk.

J3 Ludlow Mtn.
A8 Monadnock Mtn.
F3 Mt. Grant
D4 Mt. Hunger
A7 Mt. John
A8 Sable Mtn.
F1 Snake Mtn.
C6 Stannard Mtn.
C8 Stone Mtn.
J2 Tinmouth Mtn.
C3 White Face Mtn.

Lakes

B2 Arrowhead Mtn. L.
C5 Caspian L.
A6 Echo L.
A8 Great Averill Pd.
B5 Great Hosmer Pd.
C5 Hardwick L.
B7 Island Pd.
I2 L. Bomoseen
A3 L. Carmi
G2 L. Dunmore
G5 L. Fairlee
E5 L. Groton
D2 L. Iroquois
C1, G1 *Lake Champlain
A8 Little Averill L.
C8 Maidstone L.
A7 Norton Pd.
D3 Waterbury Res.
E4 Wrightsville Res.

Ski

D3 Bolton Valley
A5 Jay Peak
I3 Killington
E3 Mad River Glen
G2 Middlebury Coll.
   Snow Bowl
J4 Okemo Mtn.
I3 Pico Mtn.
C7 Q Burke Mtn.
C3 Smugglers' Notch
C3 Stowe Mtn.
F3 Sugarbush
I4 Suicide Six

State Parks

F4 Allis
B7 Brighton
H1 Half Moon Pd.
B2 Kill Kare
C8 Maidstone
C3 Smugglers Notch

Solutions

Virginia

Towns
- B3 Shenandoah Caverns
- C3 Alma
- C5 Boston
- F6 Bumpass
- C2 Cootes Store
- J7 Dinwiddie
- E3 Free Union
- G6 Goochland
- D4 Madison
- D1 Moscow
- J4 Nutbush
- A5 Paris
- I3 Red House
- H5 Sunny Side
- C3 Tenth Legion
- J5 Victoria
- A7 Vienna
- B4 Washington
- K8 Yale

Hills & Mounts
- D6 Burr Hill
- C1 Clover Hill
- K2 Crystal Hill
- A4 Fishers Hill
- B5 Flint Hill
- C7 Independent Hill
- K1 Mount Airy
- B3 Mount Clifton
- D2 Mount Crawford
- K2 Mount Laurel
- A4 Mount Olive
- D2 Mount Sidney
- D1 Mount Solon
- B4 Oak Hill
- K5 South Hill
- K2 Vernon Hill

State Parks
- H4 Bear Cr. Lake
- D8 Celedon Nat. Area
- H5 Cumberland
- H3 Holliday Lake
- G3 James River
- E6 Lake Anna
- C8 Leesylvania
- B8 Mason Neck
- H6 Pocahontas
- C7 Prince William For. Pk.
- I4 Sailor's Cr. Bfld. H.S.P.
- A4 Shenandoah R. "Andy Guest"
- A5 Sky Meadows
- K3 Staunton River Bfld.
- I4 Twin Lakes
- F8 Zoar S.F.

Villes
- B4 Bentonville
- A5 Cedarville
- H6 Clayville
- F3 Covesville
- E1 Craigsville
- I5 Deatonville
- I4 Farmville
- E5 Gordonsville
- F1 Greenville
- F5 Hadensville
- I5 Jetersville
- K6 Lawrenceville
- G1 Lowesville
- I3 Madisonville
- D3 Nortonsville
- C7 Roseville
- B5 Sperryville
- C2 Timberville
- A6 Upperville

Counties
- I5 Amelia
- D2 Augusta
- J6 Brunswick
- I2 Campbell
- E8 Caroline
- J7 Dinwiddie
- G5 Goochland
- K7 Greensville
- F7 Hanover
- H8 Henrico
- E8 King George
- D4 Madison
- I5 Nottoway
- D6 Orange
- I3 Prince Edward
- B7 Prince William
- D7 Stafford
- K8 Sussex
- A5 Warren

Washington

Towns
- F6 Seattle
- I6 Alder
- D1 Beaver
- B8 Concrete
- B5 Deer Harbor
- E1 Forks
- E8 Gold Bar
- G4 Lilliwaup
- A7 Maple Falls
- I5 Maytown
- K2 Nahcotta
- B5 Orcas
- F5 Poulsbo
- F1 Queets
- D8 Robe
- J2 Tokeland
- G4 Union
- K4 Vader
- D6 Warm Beach

Creeks & Rivers
- I4 Black
- I7 Carbon
- K5 Cowlitz
- D1 Dickey
- E4 Dungeness
- E3 Elwha
- K3 Grays
- H8 Green
- E1 Hoh
- A7 N. Fk. Nooksack
- I6 Nisqually
- C7 Pilchuck Cr.
- I7 Puyallup
- G2 Quinault
- H3 Satsop
- I5 Skookumchuck
- F7 Snoqualmie
- J3 Willapa
- H3 Wynoochee

Lakes
- J6 Alder L.
- B8 Baker L.
- I4 Black L.
- G8 Chester Morse L.
- D1 Dickey L.
- D2 L. Crescent
- C7 L. Cavanaugh
- G2 L. Quinault
- E8 L. Roesiger
- B8 L. Shannon
- H7 L. Tapps
- B7 L. Whatcom
- F7 Lake Sammamish
- G5 Mason L.
- J5 Mayfield L.
- K8 Packwood L.
- K6 Riffe Lake
- I4 Summit L.
- G3 Wynoochee L.

Mountains & Peaks
- K4 Boistfort Peak
- E4 Elk Mtn.
- D1 Ellis Mtn.
- C8 Gee Pt.
- J7 Griffin Mtn.
- C7 Haystack Mtn.
- J7 Kiona Pk.
- F3 Mt. Anderson
- A8 Mt. Baker
- E3 Mt. Carrie
- E4 Mt. Constance
- E4 Mt. Deception
- C8 Mt. Higgins
- E8 Mt. Stickney
- B7 S. Twin
- J7 Storm King Mtn.
- F4 The Brothers
- D8 Three Fingers
- J3 Walville Pk.

State Parks
- E5 Anderson Lake
- A5 Birch Bay
- C5 Deception Pass
- H7 Flaming Geyser
- C5 Ft. Ebey
- F5 Illahee
- B4 Jones Island
- K4 Lewis and Clark
- B5 Matia Island
- E5 Mystery Bay
- H7 Nolte
- G8 Olallie
- A5 Patos Island
- J4 Rainbow Falls
- C8 Rasar
- E5 Shine Tidelands
- C5 Spencer Spit
- I1 Twin Harbors
- D6 Wenberg

Washington D.C.

Towns
- E5 Rock Creek Park
- A6 Ashton
- I2 Belvedere
- K1 Chapel Acres
- F8 Defense Hts.
- A3 Emory Grove
- D6 Four Corners
- K6 Friendly
- B6 Good Hope
- A8 Hillcrest Heights
- H2 Jefferson Vil.
- I1 Kings Park
- B5 Leisure World
- E5 N. Chevy Chase
- C3 Old Farm
- A1 Quince Orchard
- H3 Seven Corners
- D1 Shady Oak
- K5 Wellington

Blvds. & Roads
- C4 Aspen Hill Rd.
- I3 Backlick Rd.
- F3 Dolly Madison Blvd.
- F4 Foxhall Rd.
- B6 Good Hope Rd.

K1	Hooes Rd.
E8	Kenilworth Ave.
A1	Long Draft Rd.
H8	Marlboro Pike
F5, G4	*Military Rd.
A3	Needwood Rd.
H6, H8	*Pennsylvania Ave.
G7	Sherriff Rd.
H3	Sleepy Hollow Rd.
B1	Turkey Foot Rd.
B8	Van Dusen Rd.

Creeks & Rivers

K2	Accotink
H7	Anacostia
D8	Beaverdam
E3	Cabin John
E1	Difficult Run
J7	Henson
K4	Little Hunting
D6	Northwest Branch
J1	Pohick
I5	Potomac
A4, E5	*Rock
K7	Tinkers

Lakes

F4	Dalecarlia Res.
E8	Greenbelt Lake
H3	L. Barcroft
B2	L. Nirvana
B2	L. Placid
G6	McMillan Res.

Golf Courses

H1, H5	*Army Navy
E2	Avenel
D3	Bethesda
D3	Burning Tree
E4	Chevy Chase
E4	Columbia
D3	Congressional
D2	Falls Road
J8	Golf Course
J4	Greendale
B7	Gunpowder
E4	Kenwood
G6	Langston
B4	Manor
B3	Needwood
A4	Norbeck
I3	Pinecrest
J1	Springfield
A5	Trotters Glen

Hills & Villes

B5	Aspen Hill
D8	Beltsville
B7	Burtonsville
H7	Coral Hills
C2	Glen Hills
F7	Hyattsville
F8	Landover Hills
F2	Lewinsville
H2	Masonville
J6	Oxon Hill
G2	Pimmit Hills
C4	Randolph Hills
A8	Scaggsville
I7	Silver Hill
B7	Spencerville
I7	Temple Hill
J4	Virginia Hills

West Virginia

Her Town

F8	Green Bank
C6	Ashley
G3	Belle
E8	Beverly
I2	Blair
E4	Chloe
F4	Coco
J4	Corinne
F6	Diana
F2	Eleanor
D4	Elizabeth
J4	Helen
G4	Jodie
E3	Kenna
H6	Leslie
I1	Myrtle
I3	Sabine
C5	Shirley
I4	Sophia

His Town

F2	Ashton
J4	Bud
G6	Calvin
A6	Cameron
H6	Carl
I5	Elton
J2	Gilbert
H2	Jeffrey
I3	Jesse
G2	Julian
E2	Leon
D5	Leopold
F1	Milton
H6	Rupert
H3	Seth
D3	Sherman
D5	Tanner
D5	Troy
G1	Wayne

Villes

D6	Churchville
E3	Cottageville
H3	Fosterville
C5	Harrisville
E8	Huttonsville
C6	Jarvisville
H1	Kiahsville
A6	Loudenville
F7	Monterville
D8	Nestorville
C3	Pettyville
J3	Pineville
B7	Rivesville
F3	Sissonville
B5	Sistersville
D7	Tallmansville
I1	Taylorville
I1	Verdunville
J6	Waiteville

State Parks

D8	Audra
H5	Babcock
H7	Beartown
H1	Cabwaylingo
E5	Cedar Cr.
H1	Chief Logan
I7	Greenbrier S.F.
G4	Hawks Nest
F7	Holly River
F7	Kumbrabow
J6	Moncove Lake
C4	North Bend
J5	Pipestem Resort
G8	Seneca S.F.
I3	Twin Falls Resort
C8	Tygart Lakes
C7	Valley Falls
H7	Watoga

Counties

E5	Braxton
E4	Calhoun
F5	Clay
D5	Doddridge
H5	Fayette
H6	Greenbrier
E3	Jackson
I2	Logan
F2	Mason
K3	McDowell
I1	Mingo
C4	Pleasants
F2	Putnam
E3	Roane
J5	Summers
B5	Tyler
E7	Upshur
B6	Wetzel
J3	Wyoming

Wisconsin

Villes

H2	Baraboo
F4	Auroraville
J3	Belleville
A3	Bloomville
C5	Clintonville
J2	Daleyville
D1	Dexterville
D8	Ellisville
C7	Flintville
E5	Greenville
F3	Harrisville
H1	Loganville
H6	Mayville
D4	Nelsonville
J2	Postville
C2	Rozellville
E4	Saxeville
D8	Stangelville
B1	Stetsonville

Rivers

G1	Baraboo
B2	Big Rib
I5	Crawfish
B3	Eau Claire
F4, K7	*Fox
F6	Manitowoc
F3	Mecan
H7	Milwaukee
B6	Oconto
E5, H1	*Pine
C3	Plover
A3	Prairie
I6	Rock
K3	Sugar
D4	Waupaca
F2	Wisconsin
D6	Wolf
J4	Yahara
E2	Yellow

State Parks

I5	Aztalan
K6	Big Foot Bch.
F2	Buckhorn
B7	Copper Culture
A2	Council Grounds
H2	Devil's Lake
I1	Governor Dodge
H8	Harrington Beach
E4	Hartman Cr.
E6	High Cliff
G8	Kohler-Andrae
F1	Mill Bluff

Solutions

G2 Mirror Lake
J2 New Glarus Woods
K6 R. Bong S.R.A.
I2 Tower Hill
K2 Yellowstone Lake

Lakes

F2 Castle Rock L.
B6 Chute Pnd.
G4 Greer L.
A7 High Falls Res.
F5 L. Butte des Morts
K6 L. Geneva
J4 L. Kegonsa
J5 L. Koshkonong
I3 L. Mendota
E5 L. Poygan
F6 Lake Winnebago
H2 Lake Wisconsin
E2 Petenwell L.
I5 Rock L.
F5 Rush L.
C6 Shawano L.

Counties

E2 Adams
F6 Calumet
G5 Dodge
C8 Door
G5 Fond du Lac
K3 Green
I5 Jefferson
F1 Juneau
K1 Lafayette
A4 Langlade
F3 Marquette
D6 Outagamie
D3 Portage
K4 Rock
H2 Sauk
B4 Shawano
A1 Taylor
K5 Walworth
H6 Washington

Wyoming

Towns

D1 Moran
J8 Albany
F7 Bar Nunn
B6 Big Horn
C7 Buffalo
H1 Cokeville
E3 Crowheart
I7 Elk Mountain
J8 Foxpark
H1 Frontier
C5 Greybull

H7 Hanna
F4 Hudson
B1 Mammoth
C4 Meeteetse
D1 Moose
D4 Owl Creek
I3 Reliance
B8 Spotted Horse
D6 Ten Sleep
C7 Ucross

Creeks & Rivers

B5, D5 *Bighorn
G3 Big Sandy
I4 Bitter Cr.
J1 Blacks Fk.
C7 Crazy Woman Cr.
F2, I2 *Green
C4 Greybull
F1 Greys
H1 Hams Fk.
I1 Little Muddy
H7 Medicine Bow
I1 Muddy Cr.
D6 Nowood
D8 Powder
C3 S. Fk. Shoshone
E7 Salt Cr.
E1 Snake
G5 Sweetwater
F4 Wind

Lakes

G7 Alcova Res.
F3 Boulder L.
E5 Boysen Res.
C3 Buffalo Bill Res.
E3 Bull L.
I8 Cooper L.
G3 Eden Res.
J2 Flaming Gorge Res.
H2 Fontenelle Res.
F3 Fremont L.
D1 Jackson L.
J8 L. Hattie
C1 Lewis L.
F2 New Fk. L.
E4 Ocean L.
G6 Pathfinder Res.
H7 Seminoe Res.
C1 Shoshone L.
F2 Willow L.
C2 Yellowstone Lake

Mountains

J7 Blackhall Mtn.
C6 Cedar Mtn.
C6 Cloud Pk.

H4 Continental Pk.
D2 Crescent Mtn.
C2 Eagle Pk.
I7 Elk Mtn.
H3 Essex Mtn.
C2 Fortress Mtn.
B3 Heart Mtn.
F1 Hoback Pk.
G8 Ice Cave Mtn.
B1 Mt. Holmes
D8 North Butte
B2 Pelican Cone
E1 Pinnacle Pk.
C4 Sheets Mtn.
B2 The Thunderer
E3 Whiskey Mtn.
D2 Younts Pk.

Counties

H8 Albany
C4 Big Horn
I6 Carbon
F5 Fremont
D4 Hot Springs
C7 Johnson
H1 Lincoln
F6 Natrona
C3 Park
B7 Sheridan
G2 Sublette
H4 Sweetwater
D2 Teton
I1 Uinta
D5 Washakie